The Activity Guide for Toddlers

171 Low Prep Toddler Activities for Sparking Creativity, Developing Motor Skills, and Having Fun Together

Table of Contents

Introduction

Did you know that 90% of brain growth happens before age 5, while the rest of the brain continues to develop until the mid-20s? Creativity plays a major role during this period of rapid growth. It nurtures the development of nerve cell connections, which are crucial for motor and fine skills.

In this book, you will find sensory play activities and understand how they contribute to a child's cognitive, physical, and emotional growth. You'll also understand how music and dance can finetune their motor skills and find activities to instill a love for art and creativity in your child. A child's creativity and blooming motor skills allow them to walk, jump, dance, run, and coordinate their hand-eye movement. Their fine motor skills are responsible for their ability to write, draw, and handle small tools. Creativity is what propels a child to put these skills to use, allowing them to develop further.

A child who is curious to paint, draw, and play using different materials and tools will experience finer and more rapid development in their fine motor skills. Children should practice using pencils, tearing, molding, and cutting in a safe environment from a young age. These activities will prepare them for fundamental life skills, such as writing, using spoons, forks, knives, and tying shoelaces. In the following chapters, you'll find a range of ideas, from energetic outdoor games to calm indoor activities, that will allow your toddler to explore their physical capabilities in a fun and safe way.

Reading to your child, playing improv games with them, and acting and creating characters together can teach them much about verbal and non-verbal communication. Chapter 5 suggests activities to unleash your toddler's imagination and ultimately inspire their love for theater, literature, and reading. These games will also improve their comprehension skills and confidence.

The activities found in this book will teach your child that nature is the best place to turn to for therapy, creativity, and inspiration. You'll find ideas you can try with your child to stimulate their observational skills and physical development in the great outdoors. They'll learn to interact with nature meaningfully, enriching their sensory experiences and boosting their mental and emotional health.

If your toddler has always been curious about the kitchen, this is your opportunity to channel their interest into experimentation and hands-on learning experiences. From involving them in cooking to creating simple chemical reactions, chapter 7 is all about having fun in the kitchen. Finally, you'll find strategies you can use to help your child develop their social skills and make the most out of their quiet time.

Chapter 1: Sensory Play and Its Benefits

Toddlers use their basic senses of smell, touch, sound, and vision to explore the world around them. Sensory play involves letting your toddler indulge in activities that stimulate their minds and assist in developing their cognitive, emotional, and social skills. These activities include using soft materials like playdough, making different sensory bags to engage their senses, water play, and much more. Sensory play lets your toddler feel different textures, sensations, and materials, allowing them to map relevant information in their brain and better navigate the world around them.

Sensory play can improve your toddler's skills.

These activities can drastically improve fine motor skills, boost problem-solving abilities, increase hand-eye coordination, and heighten their senses. By providing a safe and stimulating environment for sensory play, parents and caregivers can support toddlers' overall growth and provide them with valuable opportunities for exploration and learning.

The Importance of Engaging Your Child's Senses through Play

Introducing your toddler to sensory play can do wonders for their development. From language development to emotional growth, sensory play can directly contribute to various cognitive skills.

Language Development

Through sensory play, your toddler can increase their pace of language development. When they engage in sensory play activities, toddlers will most likely describe their feelings in their own words. They will try to associate relevant words with their sensory experiences. Parents can also engage in conversations during playtime, providing them with appropriate vocabulary and asking them open-ended questions so they can express their feelings. These activities allow your toddler to expand their vocabulary, improve communication skills, and learn to associate words with objects.

Sensory Integration

This is *the ability to process sensory information and make sense of it.* Toddlers will receive sensory inputs, which the brain will naturally process. Your toddler's senses of touch, smell, taste, and sight provide sensory data to the brain. Through sensory play, they learn to understand and interpret this information, developing a better understanding of their environment. This integration enhances their ability to focus, concentrate, and engage in tasks that require multiple sensory inputs.

Creativity and Imagination

Your child's creativity and imagination will be boosted through sensory play. At this age, letting their imagination run wild and encouraging creativity will lay the foundation for better cognitive development and increase their problem-solving skills. Parents can provide children with materials like playdough (to make different shapes) and sensory bins (shallow bins filled with rice, beans, sand, and other objects) and encourage them to use their imagination. You can create play scenarios and role-playing games that will foster their problem-solving skills, divergent thinking capability, and improved cognitive flexibility.

Sensory Regulation

Over time, sensory play aids your toddler in regulating their sensory experiences and responding accordingly. Most toddlers are hypersensitive to loud noises, whereas some children might not have problems with loud noise and require a higher sensory input to react the same way. Repeated sensory play and exposing your toddler to varying stimuli allows them to explore and understand the threshold of their senses. Understanding the limitations of their reasons enables your toddler to better manage their sensory sensitivities through self-calming activities.

Multisensory Learning

As toddlers age, their ability to create neural connections improves daily. Nurturing an environment that promotes meaningful sensory play from a young age can work wonders. With multiple senses engaged, they will develop solid neural connections, enhancing memory retention and the ability to process information better.

Cognitive Growth

Engaging your toddler in these sensory play activities is crucial for brain growth and cognitive development. Having them feel different textures, visualize colors, smell, and hear sounds allows their brains to better understand the world around them. These sensory inputs also improve problem-solving skills and enhance cognitive flexibility and critical thinking abilities. For example, when you provide your toddler with sensory bins filled with various materials, they will naturally learn to recognize how they feel and smell; then, they can categorize them in their mind. The brain connects several sensory inputs linked with the object, creating spatial awareness. Sensory play also encourages curiosity, exploration, and discovery, which foster a love for learning.

Physical Growth

Sensory play activities involve hands-on exploration, encouraging children to use fine and gross motor skills. As toddlers manipulate objects, pour, scoop, squeeze, and mold materials, they develop hand-eye coordination, fine motor control, and muscle strength. When a child engages in finger painting, they refine their fine motor skills as they grasp and manipulate the paintbrush, improving their hand and finger dexterity. Likewise, water play activities like pouring water into different containers promote hand-eye coordination and increase spatial awareness. Activities like jumping into a ball pit or crawling through a sensory tunnel promote gross motor skills and overall physical development.

Emotional Growth

Sensory play significantly impacts a child's emotional well-being. Engaging in sensory experiences allows children to regulate their emotions and provides a safe outlet for self-expression. It can be calming and soothing, reducing anxiety and stress. For example, playing with kinetic sand or squeezing stress balls can release tension and aid in managing your child's emotions. Sensory play also allows children to explore their senses and discover what they enjoy, empowering them to make choices and express preferences. This sense of control and autonomy boosts self-confidence, self-esteem, and emotional resilience.

The following are different sensory play exercises you can do with your child.

1. Sensory Bin Exploration

A sensory bin can be any soft container filled with various materials like rice, beans, sand, or water-based jelly beads. Children can interact with these materials using their hands, scoops, and small play tools. They will most likely run their fingers through, feeling the different textures, and experiment with handling these materials using pouring and scooping tools.

This stimulates their sense of touch and promotes fine motor skills as they manipulate objects.

Materials:

- Large plastic container
- Various materials (rice, beans, sand, water beads, etc.),
- Scoops
- Small containers
- Small toys

Instructions:

1. Fill the container with different sensory materials (beans, rice, etc.).
2. Place the container on a mat or towel for easy cleaning later on.
3. Let your child explore the textures, pour, scoop, and manipulate the materials using the provided tools and toys.
4. Encourage them to use their hands and fingers to feel the textures and engage in imaginative play.

2. Playdough Creations

Playdough can enhance fine motor skills.
https://www.pexels.com/photo/children-playing-with-clay-8422174/

Playdough provides a distinct sensory experience as the material can be shaped, molded, and crafted into different shapes and objects using their hands and assistive tools like cookie cutters and rolling pins. Their sense of touch activates as they squeeze, squish, and flatten the playdough. This enhances their fine motor skills, hand-eye coordination, and creativity as they transform the playdough into various objects or characters.

Materials:

- Homemade or store-bought playdough
- Cookie cutters
- Rolling pins

Instructions:

1. Provide playdough and tools to your child to create new shapes and use tools to mold objects or characters using their imagination and fine motor skills.
2. Encourage them to use their hands to mold the play dough into different shapes.
3. They can use cookie cutters to make shapes or create their own designs.
4. Let them explore the different tools and experiment with different sizes and patterns.

3. Water Play

This activity is a refreshing and exploratory experience where children can pour, splash, and play with water using different water-holding objects like funnels, sponges, and cups. They can observe the water flow, watch how the water changes as they pour it from the main container, and develop an understanding of cause and effect. You will trigger their senses of touch, sight, and sound through water play while promoting gross motor skills and hand-eye coordination.

Materials:

- Basin
- Bathtub
- Water
- Cups
- Funnels
- Sponges
- Floating toys

Instructions:

1. Set up a safe water play area using a basin or bathtub.
2. Fill it with an appropriate amount of water.
3. Provide cups, funnels, sponges, and floating toys.
4. Let your child experiment by splashing, pouring, and transferring water between containers.
5. Encourage them to use the tools to experiment with the flow of water. Make sure to supervise them at all times.

4. Sensory Bags

These soft bags are pre-filled with different materials, allowing your child to experience tactile stimulation. When your child engages with the bag, they will most likely squeeze it, manipulate it into different shapes, and map different textures and shapes in their brain. Sensory bags are particularly useful for babies and toddlers who may still put objects in their mouths as they can experience the textures and sensations safely.

Safety Guide:

Always supervise your baby or toddlers when using sensory bags, as the seal may accidentally open, allowing the objects inside to be swallowed!

Materials:

- Resealable plastic bags
- Various items for sensory stimulation (colored gel, pom-poms, buttons, small toys, etc.).

Instructions:

1. Fill the bags with different sensory items, ensuring they are tightly sealed. You can use colored gel, pom-poms, buttons, or small toys.
2. Let your child press, squeeze, and manipulate the objects inside the bag, observing textures, colors, and shapes.

5. Nature Scavenger Hunt

Going on a nature hunt allows children to engage with their surroundings and explore the sensory aspects of the natural world. They can collect items like leaves, feathers, stones, or flowers, feel the different textures, observe the colors, and smell the scents. This activity connects children with nature and encourages curiosity and observation skills.

Materials:
- Basket or container
- Nature identification guide

Instructions:

1. Take your child on a nature walk in a safe outdoor environment such as a park or garden.

2. Provide them with a basket or container to collect items from nature, such as leaves, feathers, stones, or flowers.

3. Encourage them to touch and feel the different textures, observe the colors and shapes, and smell the scents of the collected items.

4. You can use a nature identification guide to teach them about different plants and objects they discover.

6. Sensory Painting

Sensory painting stimulates the senses of touch and sight.
https://www.pexels.com/photo/person-tracing-his-hand-on-paper-8612988/

Sensory painting involves using different materials and techniques to create textured artwork. Children can use brushes, sponges, or even their fingers to apply paint, exploring different strokes and textures. They can mix colors, create patterns, and experiment with different effects. Sensory painting stimulates their sense of touch, sight, and creativity.

Materials:
- Large paper
- Non-toxic paint
- Brushes,
- Sponges

Instructions:

1. Set up a designated painting area and place a large piece of paper on the floor or table.
2. Provide non-toxic paint in various colors and brushes.
3. You can also provide sponges or encourage your child to use their fingers.
4. Let them explore different painting techniques by making brush strokes, stamping with sponges, or finger-painting.
5. Encourage them to mix colors, experiment with textures, and create unique artwork.

7. Sensory Sound Jars

Sensory sound jars are filled with small objects that produce different sounds when shaken. Children can listen to the jars and identify the sounds they hear, enhancing their auditory perception and discrimination skills. They can also experiment with combining different objects to create unique sounds.

Materials:

- Empty plastic bottles
- Various small objects (rice, dried beans, buttons, bells, etc.)

Instructions:

1. Collect empty plastic bottles of different sizes and fill them with small objects. You can fill one with rice, another with dried beans, and another with buttons or bells.
2. Make sure that the bottles are sealed tightly.
3. Encourage your child to shake the bottles and listen to the sounds produced. Discuss the differences in sounds, such as the gentle rustling of rice versus the clattering of buttons.
4. They can experiment with combining different bottles to create different auditory effects.

8. Sensory Storytime:

Sensory storybooks engage multiple senses by incorporating touch and the other senses. Children can feel different textures within the book, lift flaps, or press buttons to activate sounds. This interactive experience enhances their engagement with the story and promotes sensory exploration.

Materials:

- Storybooks with textured pages or interactive features

Instructions:

1. Choose storybooks with textured pages or interactive features that engage multiple senses.
2. Sit with your child and read the books together.
3. Encourage them to touch and feel the different textures within the book, lift flaps, or press buttons to activate sounds or other interactive elements.
4. As you read, discuss the textures and sensations they experience, and ask questions to engage them in the story.

9. Bubble Play:

Bubbles provide a visual delight and tactile sensation for children. They can blow bubbles using wands or even their hands and pop them, experiencing the texture and feel on their skin. This activity stimulates their sense of sight, touch, and hand-eye coordination.

Materials:
- Bubble solution
- Bubble wands
- Straws
- Bubble machines

Instructions:
1. Prepare a bubble solution in a shallow container or use a bubble machine.
2. Provide wands or straws for blowing bubbles.
3. Show them how to dip the wand in the solution, blow gently, and create bubbles.
4. Encourage them to chase and pop the bubbles, feeling the gentle touch of the bubbles on their skin.
5. You can also create larger bubbles by using a straw to blow through a loop of string.

10. Sensory Obstacle Course:

A sensory obstacle course incorporates various sensory elements into physical activities. Children can crawl through tunnels, balance on beams, and navigate textured surfaces. This activity promotes gross motor skills, coordination, and body awareness while engaging multiple senses.

Materials:
- Pillows
- Cushions
- Tunnels
- Balance beams
- Textured mats

Instructions:
1. Set up an obstacle course using pillows, cushions, tunnels, balance beams, and textured mats.
2. Create a path that incorporates different sensory elements. For example, place pillows on the floor for your child to crawl or jump over, set up a tunnel to crawl through, or lay down a balance beam with textured mats.
3. Encourage your child to navigate the course, engaging their senses of touch, balance, and body awareness.
4. They can explore different textures, surfaces, and movements while developing their gross motor skills and coordination.

11. Sensory Scavenger Hunt:

A sensory scavenger hunt involves finding items based on their sensory qualities, such as smooth, rough, soft, or cold. Children can search for items within their environment and collect them in a container. This activity encourages observation skills, categorization, and exploration of different sensory attributes.

Materials:

- Container for collected items

Instructions:

1. Create a list of sensory items for your child to find within your home or garden. The list can include items with specific textures or sensory qualities, such as smooth, rough, soft, or cold to the touch.

2. Give your child a container to collect the items they find. Encourage them to touch and feel each item, describing its sensory qualities.

3. Help them categorize the collected items based on their sensory attributes.

12. Sand Play:

Sand can provide a rich sensory experience.
https://www.pexels.com/photo/little-boy-playing-in-the-sand-6459/

Playing with sand provides a tactile and rich sensory experience. Children can dig, pour, and mold sand, feeling the texture and exploring its properties. They can build sandcastles, create patterns, or even bury objects to discover and uncover. Sand play stimulates their sense of touch, promotes fine motor skills, and encourages imaginative play.

Materials:

- A sandbox or tray
- Sand
- Buckets
- Shovels
- Molds

Instructions:

1. Set up a sandbox or use a large tray filled with clean sand.

2. Provide buckets, shovels, and molds for your child to dig, pour, and shape it.

3. Encourage them to use their hands to feel the texture of the sand, build sandcastles, or create patterns.
4. They can experiment with pouring and transferring sand between containers.
5. Let their imagination guide their play as they explore all the different things they can do with the sand.

13. Sensory I-Spy Bottles:

Sensory I-Spy bottles are clear bottles filled with rice or other small objects. Children can shake the bottles and locate hidden items based on sight and sound. This activity enhances visual perception, auditory distinctions, and focus.

Materials:

- Clear plastic bottles
- Rice
- Small objects
- Trinkets

Instructions:

1. Take clear plastic bottles and fill them with rice or other small objects like buttons, beads, or trinkets.
2. Make sure that the bottles are tightly sealed.
3. Show your child the bottles and discuss what objects might be hidden inside.
4. Let them shake the bottles and listen to the sounds produced.
5. Encourage them to find and identify the hidden objects by carefully turning and tilting the bottles.
6. They can engage their sense of sight and sound as they search for and locate the items.

14. Sensory Kitchen Play:

Sensory kitchen play involves providing safe food items like rice, flour, or pasta for children to explore and manipulate. They can pour, stir, and measure ingredients using different kitchen tools. This activity promotes sensory exploration, fine motor skills, and imaginative play as they pretend to cook or bake.

Materials:

- Mixing bowls
- Utensils
- Measuring cups
- Safe food items like rice, flour, and pasta

Instructions:

1. Set up a safe play area in the kitchen using mixing bowls, utensils, and safe food items like rice, flour, or pasta.
2. Let your child explore and manipulate the ingredients using their hands or kitchen utensils.

3. They can pour, stir, and measure the items, experiencing different textures and sensory qualities.

4. Encourage imaginative play by pretending to cook or bake.

5. Supervise closely to make sure they don't ingest any raw ingredients.

15. Sensory Music Exploration:

Children can engage in sensory-rich music activities by combining musical instruments with textured objects like fabric or feathers and moving to the rhythm of the music. This activity stimulates auditory perception, coordination, and kinesthetic learning while providing tactile and auditory sensory experiences.

Materials:

- Musical instruments
- Various textured objects like fabric, feathers, and bells

Instructions:

1. Provide a variety of musical instruments such as drums, shakers, or bells. Put out textured objects like fabric, feathers, or bells.

2. Play recorded music or sing songs together.

3. Encourage your child to explore musical instruments and experiment with creating sounds and rhythms.

4. They can also incorporate textured objects into their music-making by shaking or rubbing them.

5. Let them move to the rhythm of the music, feeling the vibrations and engaging their senses of sound and touch.

Chapter 2: Arts, Crafts, and Creativity

Do you remember how much you loved painting and creating things as a child? Arts and crafts are fun activities that all children enjoy. Children gravitate toward Lego, playdough, and crayons from a very young age. They don't even understand what they are, but something inside seems to drive them toward these toys! That's their creativity. This raises the question: *Are all children born creative?*

Children tend to like arts and crafts activities.
https://www.pexels.com/photo/pencils-in-stainless-steel-bucket-159644/

In 1968, NASA researched the creativity level of their engineers and scientists. Dr. Beth Jarman and Dr. George Land led this research, and the results filled them with curiosity. They wanted to find out if all people are born creative, so they used the same tests on children. They were surprised by what they discovered. A large percentage of the children scored high in the imagination category. They repeated the tests on the same children when they turned ten and found only 30% of them scored high, and another time when they were fifteen, to find that only 12% of them managed to do it again.

Dr. Jarman and Dr. Land concluded that children are creative by nature. Their creativity ends up being suppressed by either their parents or at school.

The parent's job is cultivating and nourishing this gift in their children. This chapter covers the role of arts and crafts in developing your child's self-expression, motor skills, and creativity. You will also find entertaining and artistic activities that instill a love of arts and crafts in your child.

The Role of Arts and Crafts in Your Child's Development

Your child isn't too young to learn anything. In fact, you should instill certain traits in them from a very young age. Arts and crafts play a considerable role in their development and can affect every aspect of their life.

Enhance Creativity

Children have a vast imagination, and art is the perfect outlet to express this gift and enhance their creativity. Many children develop their creativity through art, allowing them to try new things, think outside the box, and express themselves.

However, don't expect your child's drawing to be good. Parents need to differentiate between talent and creativity. Creativity isn't about doing a good job; it's about discovering, exploring, imagining, and thinking. Focus on the process and not the end result.

Improve Motor Skills

Arts and crafts involve using hands, which improves your child's motor skills and facilitates the movement of their muscles. These activities are easy and fun and give your child the freedom to do whatever they want, allowing their motor skills to develop faster. Some artistic exercises like origami, painting, and drawing can improve your child's muscle memory and hand-to-eye coordination. Once your child improves their motor skills, they can gain independence and start to eat, shower, go to the bathroom, and tie their shoelaces on their own.

Encourage Self-Expression

Children observe and take in everything that goes on around them. Some can be vocal and find it easy to express themselves about the world they are still exploring, while others can be shy and struggle with self-expression. These children need to communicate their feelings and ideas through visual outlets like arts and crafts. These activities provide them with a safe space where they feel in control and can create whatever they want using the tools of their choice.

They can also express their innermost feelings and thoughts going on in their subconscious. If you want a better idea of what goes on in your child's mind, look at what they paint or create.

Now that you know the benefits of arts and crafts in your child's development, it's time to introduce them to fun exercises to boost their creativity.

16. Making a Collage
Materials:

- Scissors
- Glue
- Paper
- Pictures of their choice

- Fabric or ribbons
- Glitter, foil, or tinsel
- Sand, feathers, leaves, or any object from nature
- Buttons, paperclips, or ice cream sticks

Safety Guide:

Be careful when your child uses scissors. Sit next to them and provide instructions. If they can't use it, either hold their hand while they are cutting (or cut for them.)

A collage will help a child express themselves.
https://pxhere.com/en/photo/773788

Instructions:

1. Place all the tools on a tray and sit with your child at a table.
2. Let them create the collage themselves and choose the tools they want to use. For instance, they might want to use paper and leaves to create a garden or a forest or use colorful paper to create a pattern.
3. Encourage and praise them at every step.
4. After they choose the pictures, either one of you can cut and stick them on the paper using glue.
5. Then, they can decorate the collage with any of the materials.

17. Playdough Creativity

Materials:

- Playdough
- Rolling pins, plastic knives, or cookie cutters
- Toys like baking equipment, cars, or plastic animals

Instructions:

1. Allow your child to experiment with the playdough a little.
2. Show them how to flatten, stretch, and roll it.
3. Hand your child different toys and encourage them to use them to create patterns or shapes.
4. You can try roleplaying games. Your child can be the baker, and you are the customer. They can make cookies with the playdough and serve them to you.
5. They can also use it to make different shapes. Let their imagination run wild.

18. Handprint/Footprint Art

Materials:

- White cardstock
- Blue cardstock
- Different colors of acrylic paint
- Paint brushes
- Scissors
- Glue
- Googly eyes
- Black marker
- Green tissue paper
- Baby wipes

Instructions:

1. Encourage your child to use the paint and the paintbrush to color their hands or feet. If they are too young, you can do it for them.
2. Then, ask them to press their hands or feet over the white cardstock.
3. Give them a wet wipe to clean and let them do it again with different paint colors.
4. Using the scissors, help your child cut off every handprint from the white cardboard and stick them with the glue on the blue cardboard.
5. Cut the green tissue paper, let your child crinkle it up, and glue it on the blue cardboard.
6. They can also add googly eyes on the hands and even draw on them to make funny faces.

Safety Guide:

Watch your child closely to ensure they don't put the paint in their mouth.

19. Paper Crown

Materials:

- Colored craft paper
- Pencil
- Scissors
- Sticky tape
- Stickers

Instructions:

1. Encourage your child to draw a zigzag in the middle of the craft paper. If they can't, hold their hand and help them out.
2. Have them cut the paper down the line and give them a hand whenever they need help.
3. Ask them to attach the two ends of the paper with sticky tape.
4. They can then decorate it with stickers.
5. Finally, they can wrap it in a circle around their head to make sure it fits before attaching it with sticky tape.

Glue here

Glue here

20. Blot Art Hearts

Materials:
- Paintbrush
- Different paint colors
- Sturdy paper
- Scissors

Instructions:
1. Since this can be tricky for your child, cut the paper into the shape of a heart. You will need about ten hearts.
2. Encourage your child to add drops of different paint colors to one side of the heart using the paintbrush.
3. They should then fold the other half of the heart over the painted side and press on it hard.
4. Then, they will unfold the card and see their beautiful creation.
5. They can repeat the previous steps with the rest of the hearts.

21. Bubble Wrap Painting

Materials:
- Paper
- Different paint colors
- Foam rollers
- Paint brushes
- Sticky tape
- Bubble wrap

Instructions:
1. Stick the bubble wrap on a table using sticky tape.
2. Using a foam roller, let your child paint over the bubble wrap with different colors.
3. There shouldn't be a lot of paint on the bubble wrap's raised surface. If there is, ask your child to roll a lighter layer.
4. Now, you or an older child should place the paper on the bubble wrap and gently press on it from the middle outwards.
5. Then, your child can remove the paper and discover the beautiful art they created.

22. Painting with Wheels

Materials:
- Paint
- Cardboard
- Drop cloths
- Car and truck toys

Instructions:

1. Your child can practice this exercise indoors or in your backyard.
2. Spread the drop cloth on the floor, then add the cardboard and the car toys.
3. Prepare the paint by putting it on paper plates, baking sheets, or pizza pans.
4. Your child should cover the cars and trucks' wheels by rolling them over the paint.
5. Now, your child can paint the cardboard by rolling the cars over them.

23. Watercolor Resist Painting

Materials:

- Liquid paint
- Watercolor paper
- Crayons
- Paintbrush

Instructions:

1. Your child can draw any shape they want using crayons on watercolor paper.
2. Next, your child will paint over the crayon drawing with the paintbrush and liquid paint.
3. Leave it to dry and hang it on your fridge to show off your little one's painting.

Suncatchers

Materials:

- Tape
- Scissors
- Contact paper
- Yarn

Instructions:

1. Your child will cut the yarn into different lengths.
2. Using sticky tape, hang the contact paper on the lower part of a window so your child can reach it.
3. Your child will then throw the yarn on the sticky paper.

Safety Guidance:

If you live on a high floor, hang the contact paper on a door instead of a window.

24. Butterfly Kite

Materials:

- Shape templates
- Markers
- Stickers
- Ribbons

- Cardstock
- Crayons
- Glue
- Long string

Instructions:

1. Draw a butterfly on the cardstock using a butterfly shape template, then cut it out.
2. Now, it's your child's turn. Instruct them to draw different simple shapes to decorate the butterfly with the black marker. Help them out if they can't draw.
3. They should then color the shapes.
4. Using glue, your child will stick the ribbon at the butterfly's end.
5. Then, they will tape the string on the top of the butterfly.
6. Your child can go out in the backyard and fly their new kite.

25. Salt Painting

Materials:

- Template of any shape
- Watercolor paper
- Water
- Food coloring
- Salt
- Glue
- Pencil

Instructions:

1. Using a pencil, help your child trace the templates over the watercolor paper.
2. Help your child add glue to outline each shape.
3. Your child should then add salt to the glue. Remove any excess salt.
4. Leave the salt and glue to dry.
5. Add a small amount of water to the food coloring to turn it into watercolor paint.
6. Place the watercolor in the pipette and give it to your child to drip slowly over the glue and salt shapes.
7. Leave it overnight to dry.

26. Paper Plate Craft

Materials:

- Googly eyes
- Patty cases
- Crayons
- Scissors

- Paper plate
- Glue

Instructions:

1. Cut the paper plate into the shape of a fish.
2. Encourage your child to decorate their fish with different colors. Let them get creative.
3. Cut the patty cases to make scales, and let your child stick them on the fish with the glue.
4. Finally, they should stick the googly eyes on the fish.

27. Paper Cup Whale

Materials:

- Marker
- Scissors
- Pipe cleaners
- Googly eyes
- Glue
- Paper
- Tape
- Paper cup

Instructions:

1. Your child will cut small parts of the paper to make the fins, then stick them to the cup's side.
2. Your child should take two small pipe cleaners, bend them a little, and tape them on the bottom of the cup to make the tail.
3. They then need to turn the cup upside down, stick the googly eyes using glue, and draw a smiley face with a marker.

28. Egg Carton Caterpillar

Materials:

- Paper
- Googly eyes
- Pipe cleaner
- Paint brushes
- Paint
- Scissors
- Egg carton

Instructions:

1. Remove the cover of the egg carton, then cut the wells along it so your child has two pieces of the same length to work with.
2. Use scissors to make two small holes in the wells at the bottom or top of the carton.

3. Now, hand the carton to your child and let them paint. They can use any color they want and do it with a paintbrush or their fingers.

4. Cut the pipe cleaner in halves and bend them slightly from one end.

5. Give the pipe cleaners to your child and instruct them to insert each one from the straight end into the holes.

6. Your child should then stick the googly eyes on the carton.

29. Fork Flower Painting

Materials:

- Plate
- Paper
- Paintbrush
- Two different color paints
- Green paint
- Forks

Instructions:

1. Pour some green paint into a small bowl or a paper plate.

2. Your child should use the paintbrush and green color to paint the bottom of the paper to create grass.

3. Your child should then paint four flowers' stems and leaves over the grass.

4. Pour the two other paint colors into two different bowls.

5. Your child should dip the top part of one fork over one of the colors, then place it over two of the drawn stems to create flowers.

6. Tell them to repeat the previous step with the second color, then place it on the other two stems.

Arts and crafts are fun; you can do all these activities with your child to encourage and bond with them.

Chapter 3: Music, Dance, Rhythm, and Creativity

In this chapter, you will learn how music, dance, rhythm, and creativity can benefit your child's confidence and overall development.

Toddlers enjoy music and dancing.

https://www.pexels.com/photo/father-and-daughter-playing-in-a-meadow-2701585/

Tap into the Rhythms of Life: Growing Your Child's Confidence and Development

Children love music. It makes them clap, jump, or shake their heads. Even when a child can barely form a word, they can respond to the sound of music. Here are five benefits of music and dancing:

1. Physical Balance

There's no better way to strengthen the mind and body than through dancing. When they dance, children learn to maintain their balance and flexibility. It also boosts their confidence, fitness level, and overall health in general.

2. Emotional Growth

Dance is an excellent way to relieve your child's stress and boost their overall mood. Try playing cheerful songs that would get them on their feet and keep them moving, for example, "Happy" by Pharrell Williams or "I Like to Move It, Move It."

3. Social Maturity

When you want to make a child socially aware and interactive, introduce them to dance activities. This would even be more fun when friends, the entire family, or a group of children their age are involved. "Kids or people, in general, tend to produce mirror neurons when they mimic the actions performed by others," according to published research from the Arts in Psychotherapy Journal. Children also tend to create a sense of attachment and social bonding when engaging with others. Dancing makes your child adopt good social skills and learn to share positive emotions with others.

4. Development in Motor Skills

Motor skills allow the use of your large and small body muscles. For example, using your hands and legs is a great way to develop your motor skills. Dancing is a brilliant way to encourage children to move their hands, legs, and body. So, whether it be clapping their hands, bending their little fingers around a tambourine, or crawling on their knees, they exercise their muscles.

5. Sensory and Creativity Development

Music is the best way to grow your child's creativity and senses. When a child dances to a rhythm, they learn to coordinate and contain their steps and actions with the provided space around them. Music helps their minds wander off to an imaginary world, but with dancing, they focus their sights on the physical world. With dance, the side of your child's brain that controls their emotions, movements, balance, memory, and images is greatly enhanced. Music is also a powerful way for children to express how they feel in creative ways, and the more they get engrossed in it, the more their creativity grows.

15 Activities to Enhance Your Child's Motor Skills and Emotional Expression

Here are 15 fun activities you can carry out with your child to build their motor skills and boost their confidence level through rhythms, creativity, music, and dance:

30. Musical Chairs

This is a classic musical activity. Each arranged chair must face the opposite side of the other. This activity is usually played with fewer chairs than the number of players; for example, if the number of players is five, there would only be four arranged chairs. This activity builds your child's self-awareness and keeps them in a position to be ready to quickly spot an empty chair.

For a less competitive game, make the number of chairs equal to the number of players. It's still a lot more fun that way too.

31. Musical Statues

This is a perfect music activity for your toddler. During a musical statue, your child learns to control their body while being asked to "freeze!" in mid-air. You play this by playing a song on your mobile phone or a CD, preferably for everyone to dance to. Then you pause the music and yell, "Freeze!" Everyone, including your toddler, must freeze immediately in their current dancing positions just as you pause the song. This would be so much fun for children when they all freeze together without any of them being disqualified.

32. What Instruments Do You Hear?

This game aims to teach listening with precision as you name the instruments you hear. To make it fun, ensure your child knows a range of musical instruments and how they sound. If you don't have any musical instruments around the house, you can play videos of them on YouTube.

33. Creating Homemade Musical Instruments

When looking for a way to draw your child's attention, try telling them about making one great musical instrument. Your child would not only want to make those instruments with you, but they'll also look forward to playing them. This builds your child's motor skills, creativity, and a good social and emotional bond with you. There are a variety of homemade musical instruments you can learn and make with your child:

- A tin can drum

- Paper straw panpipes

- An elastic band guitar

Starting a family band with these tools would be a great way to build bonds with your child and those around you. Children love it when they can make so much noise with drums, tambourines, and panpipes, especially those they crafted themselves.

PLASTIC EASTER EGG MARACAS

NEEDED MATERIALS:

Plastic Easter eggs

Plastic spoons

White tape

Popcorn kernels

Markers

DIRECTIONS:

1. Fill the eggs with popcorn kernels.

2. Tape two plastic spoons on either side.

3. Tape the spoon ends together.

4. Decorate the tape with markers.

BALLOON SKIN DRUMS

NEEDED MATERIALS:

Small tin cans
Balloons
Scissors
Ribbon
Paint and brush
Craft or hot glue

DIRECTIONS:

1. Wash, dry, and remove labels from the tin cans.
2. Paint can and/or decorate as desired.
3. Cut the balloon and stretch it over the tin can's opening.
4. Add ribbon to the seam of the balloon to help seal it in place and for decoration.

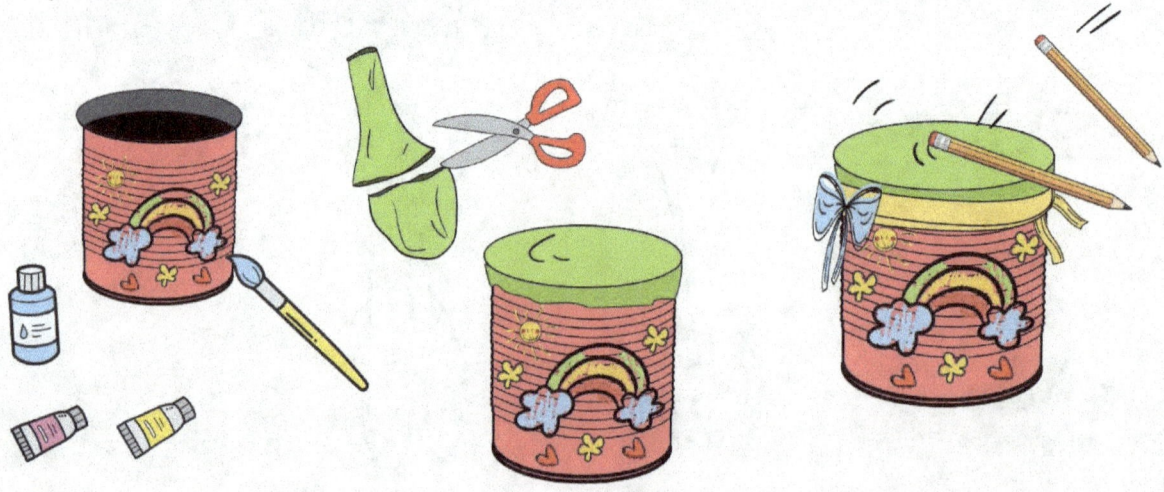

Popsicle Stick Harmonica

NEEDED MATERIALS:

two popsicle sticks

two rubber bands

two toothpicks cut the width of the popsicle stick

Paper (popsicle-sized strip)

DIRECTIONS:

1. Place paper strip between popsicle sticks.

2. Wrap a rubber band snugly around one end.

3. Place a toothpick inside the rubber band.

4. Put the other toothpick at the other end of the popsicle sticks and wrap it with the other rubber band.

Singing Straws

NEEDED MATERIALS:

six to eight straws

Sticky tape

Scissors

Colored paper (optional)

DIRECTIONS:

1. Cut the straws into different lengths in groups of two.

2. Cut a long piece of sticky tape and place the straws on the sticky side in twos, arranging them from shortest to longest.

3. Secure in place with additional tape.

4. Decorate with colored paper (optional).

34. Musical Packages

In this game of patience, items are wrapped with many layers of a newspaper sheet. They are then passed around to each participant of the game. Each person must unwrap a layer of the cover and pass it to the other person. It goes around like that in a circle until the last layer is unwrapped. Add a musical instrument like an egg shaker inside the wrap to make this more fun. This would build momentum and curiosity. Whichever child unwraps the final later gets to keep what's inside.

35. Party Freeze Song

Play a song and encourage your child to dance. The catch here is that they have to stop whenever you say so. Remember that these games depend on your child's age, which would determine their response. You should make a few demonstrations before they get the hint of it. This type of game sharpens listening and develops impulse skills. Say "stop" and then "dance" from time to time, and have them enjoy the fun of it.

36. Matching Sounds

You can start with pairs of homemade instruments. When you play an instrument, the goal is for your child to listen and search for something that can make the closest sound possible. Here are a few examples:

- A triangle produces a faint or sharp sound. Two spoons can make such a sound.
- Drums produce a deep sound. A box can make that sound, too.
- Cymbals produce a sharp sound. A pot lid can also do this.

There are no rules to playing this game. One person makes the suggested sound, and the other player goes looking.

37. Mimicking Steps

Here, all you need to do is to create a dance step while playing music and ask everyone, including your child, to repeat your moves. Do this game in turns and see how creative and fun it gets.

38. A Little Elephant

With this song, you can teach your child how to count and make sense of basic numbers. You can even take advantage of this opportunity and teach how to walk in a straight line. To play, place a string on the ground and begin by walking on it, using your arms for balance. Then, everyone can sing the lyrics together.

39. Draw Your Music

You'll need a large piece of paper and drawing pencils or crayons. Play a song and ask them to draw what they feel or hear. It could be a wavy line, a zigzag line, or a curved line. Make this an open-ended activity, and watch your children express themselves through what they hear. Make sure to draw yours as well.

40. Hide, Listen, and Spot

This game involves hearing sounds and guessing where they came from.

In this game, one of you is going to be blindfolded. The aim is to figure out where the sound is coming from. To play, blindfold your child and use whatever you have on hand, whether an instrument or household items, to produce sounds. Do that while moving away from them. When you get as far away as possible, hide and keep making sounds. Once you stop, that's their signal to come looking for you.

41. Sock Puppet Show

You can teach your child how to use a puppet to create a show. You can use various characters to play roles and express different emotions. The best part about this activity is that they can take as long as they want to create the puppets.

CROCODILE PUPPET

1. Cut the foot of a sock as shown. Turn sock inside out.

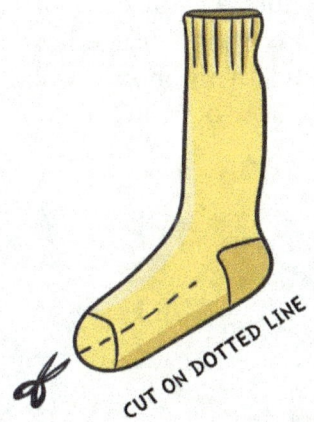

CUT ON DOTTED LINE

2. Cut a piece of red material in the shape of the opening and sew to sock with an overhand stitch.

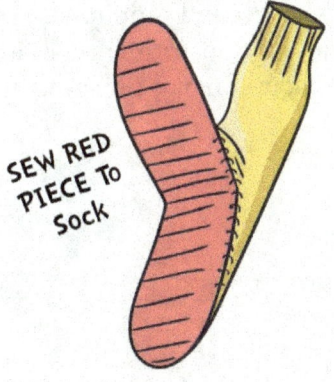

SEW RED PIECE TO SOCK

3. Turn sock right side out. Cut cardboard the same size as the red mouth. Fold and insert in sock.

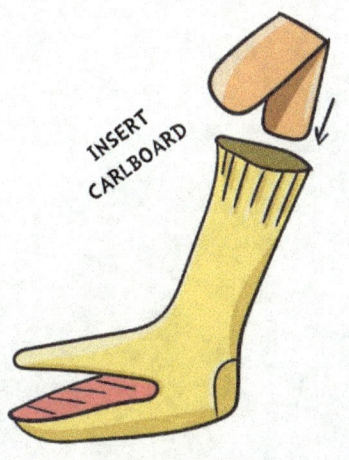

INSERT CARLBOARD

4. Add buttons for eyes and nose. Use yarn braids and curls for hair.

42. Dancing Scarves

Dancing with colorful scarves and ribbons opens up your child's imagination. It also builds their motor skill as they wave and move the scarfs around. To make this even more interesting for them, find rainbow scarves or ribbons and watch them swirl them around for what feels like ages. You can make a video and take pictures of them as they do this.

43. Marching to a Beat

Teach your child how to dance to the beats of a song by making certain gestures with their feet and hands. Show them how to lift their legs and arms high above the ground and back onto the floor, following the rhythm of the beats.

44. Head, Shoulders, Knees, and Toes

This activity is for children who can't keep still. Sing or talk "Head, Shoulders, Knees, and Toes" and move both your hands accordingly and have the child do the same.

The best way to bring out the creativity in your child is through music, dance, and rhythm. To improve your child's health and emotional growth, you can have them engage in activities like musical chairs, creating homemade instruments, matching sounds, and many more. Make the most of your time with your children, and make precious memories that will last you a lifetime.

Chapter 4: Let's Get Physical

This chapter is about fun activities that boost your toddler's physical development. You will never run out of options to keep your child happy and engaged.

As a parent, watching your little one grow and explore the world is one of the most rewarding parts of the job. Their energy seems boundless at this age, and you want to keep them active and engaged most of the time, which is the key to managing all that energy. The activities in this chapter are designed for toddlers - they're fun and creative and help build crucial skills like balance, coordination, and motor skills. Whether you're looking for an energetic outdoor game or a calm indoor activity for your child, this chapter has you covered.

Children tend to enjoy the outdoors.
https://www.pexels.com/photo/father-and-kid-on-terrace-with-picturesque-view-3932948/

Benefits of Outdoor Play vs. Indoor Play

Whether indoor play suits your taste better than outdoor play (or vice versa), the point to be made here is that the interest of the children comes first. Outdoor play offers a lot of benefits to children compared to indoor play.

Outdoor play makes room for more physical activities, which, in turn, allows children the opportunity to develop gross motor skills and improve their overall health. It also brings children closer to natural elements, like making contact with the sand to build sand castles or dig a ditch, thus helping them develop an appreciation for the environment. Interaction with nature also has a way of enhancing creativity, cognitive development, and problem-solving skills. This could be seen as a result of them trying to find new ways to build and decorate better sand castles.

Additionally, outdoor play encourages healthy self-esteem, social interaction, and teamwork, as outdoor recreation makes children engage in group activities and games to sometimes achieve a common goal. Being accepted among peers during such activities helps build a sense of belonging and appreciation for themselves.

Indoor play also has its advantages too. One such advantage includes creating a controlled environment for certain activities that don't necessarily need to be outdoors. Such activities include Lego-building, and this activity in itself fosters great imaginative play regardless of weather conditions.

Fun Outdoor Games for Children

At their age, toddlers are always eager to go outdoors. They are constantly curious about the world around them and want to explore it. So, getting them outside is always a great idea for more reasons beyond just *fun*. Getting outside with your toddler will also help them develop physically and mentally while having fun at the same time. These outdoor activities have a way of helping your child build up essential skills that they can quickly implement in school and other social situations. Also, it is no news that having your children play outside, in the warm sun and the cool breeze, has a lot of health benefits for them.

Here are some engaging outdoor games that have been put together to make your little one laugh, learn, and have fun.

45. **Obstacle Courses:** Set up a simple obstacle course in your backyard with hula hoops to jump in and out of, balls to crawl under, balloons to pop, and tunnels to crawl through. This builds balance, coordination, and motor skills.

46. **Bubble Blowing:** Bubbles are endlessly entertaining for toddlers and develop their hand-eye coordination and motor skills. Show your toddler how to gently blow into a bubble wand to make bubbles. Have them dip the wand in the solution, raise it to their mouth, and blow gently but steadily to produce a stream of bubbles. Make a challenge out of seeing who can blow the biggest bubble.

47. **Hopscotch:** Use chalk to draw a hopscotch board on the sidewalk. Have your toddler hop, jump, and balance as they go through the numbers. This helps with balance, motor skills, and counting.

48. **Catch and Release:** Gently toss a ball, beanbag, or other soft toy back and forth with your toddler. Start close together and slowly move further apart as their skills improve. This helps hand-eye coordination and motor skills.

49. **Follow the Leader:** Walk, run, hop, jump, spin, march, and have your toddler imitate your movements. Switch who plays leader now and then. This builds motor skills, balance, and coordination.

Being outside with your little one provides opportunities for learning and development while having fun. These simple activities will keep your toddler engaged and build crucial skills. Most of all, make sure to enjoy the special time together outside in nature.

Exciting Indoor Activities

Outdoor activities are great, but due to season changes, clashing schedules, and work, they're just not possible sometimes. The goal is to keep your toddler happy and always engaged—the where and how are unimportant as long as your child is excited and happy.

Indoor activities are a great way to stimulate your little one on rainy or chilly days. Having your toddler spend so much time inside might seem dreadful initially, but it can be an opportunity to bond. Toddlers have the energy to burn, so providing outlets to explore their physical skills indoors is vital for their development and your sanity! Here are some excellent indoor exercise options:

50. **Obstacle Courses:** If you can't set one up outside, you can do it inside. Set up a simple course with hula hoops, tunnels made from chairs, blankets, and pillows to crawl through, balls to roll and throw, and targets to aim for. You can even give your toddler the chance to be creative and have them design the course.

51. **Puzzles:** Have your toddler exercise their problem-solving, cognitive, and creative muscles with puzzles. This will sharpen their minds and allow them to have fun indoors. Completing the puzzle also instills a sense of accomplishment and pride, boosting their confidence levels for other tasks. You can get a store-bought puzzle or have them draw their own. That will put their creativity to the test. They can use a sturdy cardboard piece or a Bristol board.

52. **Stringing Items Together:** Stringing beads, pasta, cereal, or buttons together on yarn or string develops fine motor skills and hand-eye coordination in a fun, engaging way. Provide different-sized items for your toddler to manipulate and let them be creative in designing their necklaces or bracelets. Give them laces or strings and large wooden or plastic beads with holes big enough to fit through. Show them how to thread the lace through the bead hole and pull it through. Have them practice stringing the beads onto the lace. Start with larger beads, then progress to smaller ones as their skills improve. Display their creations proudly to motivate them to keep practicing.

53. **Play Music and Have a Dance Party:** Toddlers love moving to music. Put on some upbeat songs and dance together. Spin, jump, march, clap along - any energetic, full-body movements. Dancing also helps with balance, coordination, and body awareness.

54. **Hide and Seek:** This list will be incomplete without hide and seek to balance things. You and your child can take turns hiding and looking for one another around the house. To make it more fun, other family members can join in.

55. **Indoor Bowling:** Save time and the earth by using your old recyclable bottles to create a makeshift bowling set. Your indoor bowling rink is done by lining up 6 to 10 water bottles in your living room or at the end of the hall and taping the area to be used as the starting line. You can use cardboard boxes as bumpers as well. Grab an indoor ball, preferably medium-sized, and you are all set to bowl.

If the bottles don't stay fixed, adding some water will help you stabilize them. Just remember to screw the cap tightly to avoid any spills. You can purchase children's indoor bowling kits if you want something more practical.

56. Simon Says: The classic game of Simon Says is ideal for helping toddlers follow basic instructions and learn body awareness. Give simple commands like "Simon says jump up and down" or "Simon says touch your nose." Toddlers must follow the commands when you say, "Simon says," and not follow commands without that phrase. This game helps toddlers develop listening skills, understand the meanings of words for different body parts and movements, and control their bodies.

57. Hot Potato: This is another fun activity to get them all excited and giggling. You only need a softball or a bean bag, acting as the hot potato, to start things. While everyone sits in a circle, music is played in the background as you take turns passing the item as fast as possible to the person next to them. Anyone holding the potato when the music stops is eliminated. Keep at it until there is only one player left.

58. Touch-and-Feel Box: This game will have your child making all the strangest faces; you do not want to miss it! Also, it is a great way to improve their sensory skills. For this game, you will need a shoe box or any other box with a lid. Make a hole the size of your child's hand on one side of the box, place an item in it, and cover it with the lid. Have your child put their hand through the hole you made to guess what you set in the box. This will keep your child's mind sharp and active as they try to determine what you have placed in the box. You can also make it more fun by asking them questions about the item or dropping clues to help them.

With just some simple props and enough enthusiasm, these indoor activities will have your toddler giggling, moving, and mastering new skills in no time. They also provide opportunities for bonding and joyful interaction between you two.

Developing Motor Skills through Play

Playtime is a learning opportunity for toddlers. Their bodies and minds are developing rapidly, and playing builds the motor skills and coordination they'll use for the rest of their lives.

Outdoor Play

Riding a tricycle can strengthen your toddler's leg muscles.
https://www.pexels.com/photo/boy-riding-green-bike-1058501/

Playing outside gives toddlers the chance to strengthen their muscles and improve balance. This includes activities like:

59. **Going to the Playground:** Swings, slides, and climbing structures build leg and core strength.

60. **Playing with Balls:** Throwing, kicking, and chasing balls improve hand-eye coordination and balance.

61. **Riding Tricycles:** Pedaling strengthens leg muscles and improves motor skills. Look for tricycles with handrails for support.

62. **Playing Make-Believe:** Pretending to be animals walking on all fours, jumping like frogs, or flying like birds builds muscle control and flexibility.

Indoor Play

There are lots of fun indoor activities for developing motor skills:

63. **Building Blocks:** Stack blocks and knock them down. This helps with coordination and grasping.

64. **Treasure Hunts:** Treasure hunts are an excellent way to build motor skills. Prepare a list of items and matching clues to help them out when searching.

65. **Dancing and Moving to Music:** Put on some fun children's music and move together. Dancing improves balance, sense of rhythm, and flexibility.

66. **Playing with Shape Sorters:** These toys help toddlers learn how to manipulate objects and fit them into the proper spaces. Great for developing fine motor control and hand-eye coordination.

The goal is to keep them active and engaged. Combining structured activities with free, self-directed play allows toddlers to strengthen their bodies and build new skills at their own pace.

Safety Tips and Guidelines

When your children are playing, there are some safety precautions to keep in mind:

- **Adult Supervision:** You always want to keep an eye on your child during these activities, especially if your toddlers are between the ages of 1 and 3.

- **Age-Appropriate Materials:** Make sure that the materials you use in the activities are age-appropriate and safe for your child.

- **Safe Play Environment:** Work hard to create a safe play environment for your toddler by removing potential hazards or obstacles. Secure cords, keep electrical outlets covered and ensure all the furniture or play equipment is stable and secure. If you are outdoors, do the same, and make the area free from harmful objects or substances.

- **Hygiene and Cleanliness:** Maintain your child's hygiene and cleanliness during sensory activities involving food, water, or sensory bins. Their hands and materials must be clean to prevent the spread of germs.

- **Allergies and Sensitivities:** Be aware of any allergies or sensitivities your child may have, especially when engaging in activities involving food, materials, or outdoor environments. Be careful and avoid allergens or irritants that may cause harm or discomfort to your toddler.

Remember, these safety tips are general guidelines, and assessing the specific activity and environment is essential to ensure the child's safety.

15 Easy Exercises for Toddlers

Below are more exciting activities for you and your toddler to keep things fresh and fun! These activities can be played both indoors and outdoors:

67. **Water Play:** Use tubs, buckets, and other containers to splash and pour water.

68. **Musical Instruments:** Musical instruments like shakers, drums, and xylophones will allow your toddler to experiment and develop their creativity.

69. **Sensory Art:** Help them explore textures and materials like playing with playdough or paints.

70. **DIY Sensory Bottles:** If you are looking for an excellent way to stimulate your child's visual and auditory senses, creating sensory bottles using water, glitter, small toys, beads, etc. is a good way!

71. **Balloon Play:** Engage in activities like balloon volleyball.

72. **Pretend Play:** By encouraging imaginative play with pretend kitchens, doctor kits, or dollhouses, you get to build your child's creative imagination.

73. **DIY Instruments:** Help them create simple instruments using household items like rice-filled bottles or rubber band guitars.

74. **Indoor Camping:** Set up a cozy blanket fort, read books, or play with flashlights.

75. **Sorting Games:** Improve your child's senses by using objects like colored blocks or shapes and sort by color, size, or shape.

76. **Bean Bag Toss:** Create targets using hula hoops or buckets and make it a fun game by having them toss bean bags into them.

77. **DIY Sensory Board:** Make a sensory board with different textures, buttons, zippers, and Velcro for exploration.

78. **Outdoor Nature Art:** Create beautiful natural outdoor artwork by using items like leaves and flowers.

79. **Color Scavenger Hunt:** Take scavenger hunting up a notch by helping them find objects of different colors around the house or outdoors.

80. **Play With Scarves:** Give them colorful scarves for them to wave, throw, and catch.

81. **Water Sponge Play:** Give them sponges and a bucket of water for squeezing and soaking up water. This simple process will keep your toddler engrossed and fascinated.

With these engaging exercises, toddlers can build their physical abilities through interactive play. Parents should supervise activities and provide guidance to keep things fun and avoid frustration. Starting simple and progressing as skills improve will help your toddler gain confidence in their movements and balance over time. Keep mixing the activities between energetic and calm, indoor and outdoor. The key is to make physical activity a fun and regular part of your toddler's day. Now get out there and play! Your toddler will thank you for it, and you'll both get to build great memories of your time together.

Chapter 5: Reading and Acting

Kids are naturally creative, curious, and imaginative. They like to think outside of the box and explore their surroundings. They are also very sensitive to their environment. Everything they observe, hear, or come into contact with leaves a mark of some kind. Acting and reading activities will allow your child to view others and the world differently. Improv offers a creative outlet for self-expression and serves as a safe and fun learning experience.

Reading with your toddler can improve their reading and language skills.

The activities in this chapter will improve your child's reading and language abilities and expose them to the beauty of acting and performance. These exercises will work wonders for their confidence and motor skills as well. This chapter delves into the magical effects of story-telling, reading, and acting on a child's imagination, creativity, and understanding. Doing these activities with your child is a surefire way to foster their love for books and the world of theater.

Benefits of Reading and Acting

Reading and acting skills can improve your child's social skills and teach them to interact with others. Improv teaches children to look for shared interests with people, search for creative and interesting conversation openers, and unleash their imagination. Understanding how to make friends and build relationships from a young age will set them up for success later in life.

Interactive reading, acting, and improv incorporate physical activities that encourage children to coordinate their brains, eyes, and movements, which improve their motor skills and increase their self-reliance. Reading new books, creating stories, using props, and learning lines will also expand your child's vocabulary and teach them to learn new tools. This might help them develop reading and writing skills sooner.

You should also consider trying these exercises with large groups of people to improve your child's confidence. Acting, self-expression, and public speaking will teach your child to be comfortable in front of a large crowd. This skill will benefit them significantly in professional and academic settings.

Teaching your child to think in new and unconventional ways will make their lives easier as adults. Complex problems require creative solutions, and there is no better way to improve their problem-solving skills than through reading and improv. These activities expose your child to a wide array of scenarios that will encourage them to express themselves and work their way innovatively through challenges. Since most of the activities in this chapter require at least two people, they will also learn the importance of teamwork and understand how to work effectively with others to achieve the best results.

The following improv and reading exercises will test your child's creativity and imagination while enhancing their emotional intelligence, comprehension skills, empathy, attention to detail, and self-confidence. You can do these exercises alone with your child, but they're much more fun when done in groups. Most of these games can be enjoyed by adults as well. You can get the entire family involved!

82. Use Unconventional Props

In this improv game, your child should use any object around the room to create a skit. Encourage them to use the item in an unconventional way other than its intended use. This exercise aims to get your child to channel their creative thinking skills to be as unexpected and funny as possible. For instance, they might use a kitchen bowl as a hat or a shoe as a smartphone.

83. Character Impersonation

This challenges children's contemplation, analysis, and application skills. They need to consider all the characteristics of the character that they'll impersonate, from tone and expression to appearance and behavior, to integrate them into their performance. Cut up small pieces of paper, writing the name of a movie or cartoon character that your child knows on each one. Remember that the characters you choose must have distinctive and unique characteristics.

Place the pieces of paper into a bowl and ask your child to draw a name. Anyone who isn't playing can assist the child with reading the character's name. The other players will have to guess the character based on their impersonation. For instance, if they received Cinderella, they can integrate a broom, toy birds, or slippers into their performance.

84. Animal Impersonation

This exercise is designed to get children to think about body language and non-verbal communication. Even though this can be challenging for a toddler, they'll try to figure out how an animal's movements and behaviors can capture its essence.

Ask your child to choose an animal and keep the choice to themselves. They should then try to mimic the animal's behavior for other players to guess. Make sure to take turns so your child gets a chance at guessing. Guessing encourages them to work on their interpretation, inferential, and attention skills.

85. Group Story-Making

Making a story in pairs or as a group requires anyone involved to use their collaboration, creativity, and listening skills. The game begins with the first player saying the story's opening line. The following person then says another logical line to the story. The players keep taking turns, building on the narrative until the story ends. Work together to make the story as coherent and enjoyable as possible, incorporating a problem and resolution to the narrative. You can write each line down or use your phone to record the game to read the final result out loud when you're done.

86. Make Assumptions

This will encourage your child to explore their imagination and read body language. If done often enough, it can help them develop a sense of empathy. They'll also learn that there are always untold stories and reasons behind people's actions and behaviors. Observe passers-by whenever you and your child are out, and start making assumptions about them.

Think about where they came from, where they're going, what they like doing in their free time, what they do for a living, and whether they have a family. Observe their facial expressions and body language, creating background stories for them. For example, if you see a woman in formal attire with a frown, you might assume she got demoted or fired. Remember to keep your voices lowered so you don't accidentally offend someone.

87. Choose Someone to Imitate

If your child has a favorite actor, search for one of their scenes on YouTube and show it to them. Experiment with ways to imitate their body language, tone, emotions, and voice together. If they don't have an actor in mind, watch a movie together. When you're done, have them choose their favorite character. You can also choose yours so you can both recreate your favorite scenes. You don't need to copy everything they do. However, you should try to get them to focus on the details, like mannerisms, how they talk, and even their walk. That is the whole purpose of the exercise.

Impersonation makes anything more fun.
Scott Barlow, (CC BY-NC-ND 2.0) <https://creativecommons.org/licenses/by-nc-nd/2.0/>
https://www.flickr.com/photos/barl0w/2983543259

88. Copying Roles

This exercise will get your child thinking about how different people act based on their roles. It will also enhance their emotional awareness over time. Each profession requires a different tone of voice, range of emotions, body language, and energy. Your child will try to copy three roles they're familiar with; for example, teacher, police officer, and scientist. Set a timer, asking them to improvise for 30 to 40 seconds before shifting to the next one.

89. Simplified Pictionary

While Pictionary is best played in groups, you can play it alone with your child. Write simple words on pieces of paper and put them in a bowl. Ask someone who isn't playing to assist your child with reading the term when it's their turn. They will then draw a word for you to guess what it is. Take turns, giving your child the opportunity to guess.

PICTIONARY WORDS

Shoe	Fish	Rooster	Egg
Door	Sandwich	Dress	Bird
Trash Can	Cookie	Aeroplane	Octopus
Christmas Tree	Socks	Bubbles	Star
Television	Book	Ocean	Coffee
Moon	Pants	Ball	Apple
Eyes	Happy	Banana	Mailbox
Spider	Roof	Butterfly	Nose
Snow	Candy	Cupcake	Tree
Drum	Skateboard	Rainbow	Cat
Shirt	Sun	Grapes	Leg
Sad	Water	Pizza	Lips
Doll	Bed	House	Cloud
Cup	Hat	Sleep	Orange

90. Interactive Movement Books

Interactive movement books can improve a child's motor and comprehension skills. Read books that incorporate physical activity and are suitable for your child's age. Opt for books that encourage children to move around and use positional concepts. This way, when the text says, "on the table," your child can point to or touch the surface of a table.

If the book incorporates action words, such as "run, "clap," or "jump," your toddler can do these actions. For example, if the book mentions the color red, you can ask them to quickly find something red in the room. Get as creative as possible to engage your toddler in the story-telling process.

91. Set a Word Limit

Ask your child to think of a concept or object they can explain in 1 to 10 words. For example, if they think of the moon, they can say round, sky, night, and shine. Take turns so both of you can get a chance to explain and guess.

92. Use the Last Letter

Play a word game where you can only say one word, starting with the last letter of the word the other player used. To make the game more educational, you can set a theme for the exercise that aligns with the concepts that your child is learning in preschool. If they're learning about countries, for example, you can go: "France," "Egypt," "Tanzania," etc.

93. Get Moving

This is one of the easiest and most fun improv exercises toddlers can do. It requires no verbal communication, making it suitable for children who can't yet think on their feet. One person can call out pairs of things, such as lock and key, for the other to depict them using only their body.

94. Mimic the Emotions

This game can improve a child's emotional awareness and cultivate their sense of empathy. Initiate a conversation with your child, expressing several emotions throughout. If you show excitement, your child should attempt to portray that emotion and copy your body language as if staring at a mirror. Their emotions and facial expressions should shift as you shift to anger, sadness, or a neutral expression.

95. Space Jump

This fun exercise will test your child's reactivity and critical thinking skills. Ask your child to act out any scene they desire. You should then shout "space jump" whenever you want them to freeze in place. The second player should get into the first player's frozen position (your child, in that case) before starting their scene. The whole point here is to freeze as soon as the words "space jump" are said while thinking of a very challenging position to baffle the other player.

96. Consider the Environment

This is yet another non-verbal improv game that will get your child's creative juices flowing. One player should secretly think of a setting and act how they would if they were actually there. For instance, they must act frightened yet excited if they're pretending to be at a theme park or pretend they're shopping if they think of the mall. The player must think of a tricky setting to make it harder for others to guess.

Improv and reading games can offer many benefits and entertainment for children and adults alike. These exercises will not only strengthen your bond with your child, but they'll also strengthen your language, communication, critical thinking, and problem-solving skills. Reading and improv exercises will teach your child much about others and the world around them, allowing them to cultivate a more profound sense of understanding, acceptance, and empathy.

Chapter 6: Exploring Nature

Nature is the finest teacher your toddler can ever have. It is one of the oldest forms of sensory-motor development for children. After all, before the birth of civilization, only nature existed in its raw, unrestrained glory. Apart from sensory motor skills, your child can learn and experience the science of exploring, the art of paying attention, the thrill of taking risks, and develop fine and gross motor skills. With every new thing they learn, their confidence will grow, and their social skills will improve. Needless to say, they will acquire several physical skills along the way.

More importantly, your toddler will learn to appreciate nature. Today, when computers and smartphones are ruling people's waking hours and exciting new gadgets are being invented every week, affinity and love for nature are rapidly declining. How often do you stand and feel the grass beneath your feet, stop and smell the flowers strewn in your front yard, or wait to observe a caterpillar transform into a butterfly?

Since your child will develop a love for nature at a very young age, the bond will stay with them for years ahead. And when they grow up, you might just find them going to explore the great outdoors from time to time!

Ideally, you can leave your toddler to crawl or run free on your lawn or in a nearby park. They will develop all the skills above on their own. But the best way to go about it will be with the aid of outdoor activities. It is more fun and educational, and you can also become a part of their sensory growth regime. Here are a few exciting ways of exploring nature with your toddler.

97. Collect Rocks, Leaves, and Twigs

Collecting rocks with your toddler can be a form of sensory play.

Your toddler's curiosity will lead them to touch every new thing they see. And the most prominent things that they see in nature are rocks, leaves, and twigs. These come in many shapes, colors, sizes, and textures. Two major senses come into action here: sight and touch.

Start off small. Show them how to grasp a rock and bring it to you. Then, ask them to bring another rock and then another. Let them observe its texture and feel its form. Is it circular? Let them feel its shape. Show them other similarly shaped rocks and ask them to bring you more. Progress to the color of the rock. Is it black? Ask them to bring more black-colored rocks.

Understanding textures may be slightly more difficult for them. But texture contrast won't be hard to grasp once they can differentiate between colors and shapes. You can conduct a similar activity with leaves and twigs. Encourage them to keep a collection of these things, then show them how to sort them according to shapes, sizes, colors, and textures.

98. Color Scavenger Hunt

Now that they can understand the difference between various shapes, sizes, colors, and textures, you can progress to a slightly more difficult yet interesting activity: a scavenger hunt. Perceiving different colors is one of the easiest things for toddlers; thankfully, nature is ripe with objects of various colors. All you need is an item list.

Start with the primary colors: red, green, and blue. Your child will be effortlessly able to distinguish between these. Here's how you can prepare for the hunt.

1. Draw three squares, one below the other, on a plain white piece of paper.
2. Fill the first square with green (easiest to find in nature), the second with red, and the third with blue.
3. Show them how to bring a green-colored leaf and place it on the green square and red and blue colored fruit/flower on the respective squares.
4. Ask them to do the same on their own.

    Over time, you can move on to other colors found in nature.

99. Universal Scavenger Hunt

Expand your item list to other things found in nature. Draw a leaf, rock, twig, butterfly, worm, flower, fruit, etc. You can't expect your child to bring every little thing on their own (butterflies are tough to catch!), so help out wherever necessary.

Scavenger hunts improve your toddler's observation and memory retention. Plus, it is much more fun to match colors, shapes, objects, etc., in nature than merely on a piece of paper.

100. The Natural Sandbox

You don't need a special sandbox when you can give your child a natural one. Take them to the beach, or let them dig up garden soil. Provide an incentive by hiding small toys like squishy ducks and slinkies beneath the surface. Digging not only strengthens their palms but also stimulates their sense of touch.

101. Wet and Dry Sorting

Another basic way to improve your child's touch sense is to make them understand the difference between wet and dry. Take them to a nearby lake and place two boxes of different colors (say black and white) in front of them. Pick up a wet pebble and place it in their hand, then ask them to drop it in the black box. Place a dry pebble in their hand to drop into the white box. Let them repeat this exercise by themselves and behold the joy on their face when both boxes are filled!

102. Smelling Flowers and Tasting Fruits

Tasting fruits can introduce toddlers to new food items.

This is an upgraded version of the scavenger hunt. Once your child can match the pictures of fruits and flowers in a book to the actual object, you can have them smell the flowers and taste the fruits. Now, keeping the picture book open, hide the flowers and fruits. Remove one petal from each flower and chop a tiny part of each fruit. Ask them to smell the flower or taste the fruit and have them point out the right flower or fruit in the picture book.

Start with only two flowers or two fruits at first. They may get it wrong a few times, but as their senses of smell and taste get used to the activity, they will get it right eventually.

103. Playdough in Nature

Textures are often hard to memorize by touch alone, not just for children but for adults, too. That is where modeling dough comes in. Ask your child to press different kinds of rocks in the dough. That way, they can see the texture while feeling it with their hand, making it easier to memorize. Then, you can play a scavenger hunt with them using textures as clues!

104. Snow or Mud Creations

Making a snowman with your toddler can teach them different shapes.

It is fun for toddlers to play in the snow or mud. But it is even more exciting for them to create stuff with snow or mud. It's a natural version of playdough. Start with simple things. Show them how to create a ball. Progress to a snowman or mudman, followed by basic shapes like mountains and walls. Let their imagination run wild after that.

105. Nature Art

So far, your little one may have drawn random shapes on paper or created paint impressions of indoor objects. It's time to take their creativity outside. Let them play with crayons or paint on a blank paper while sitting in your backyard. You may notice a difference in their indoor scrawls and outdoor ones. The latter may be slightly more artistic. That is their imagination!

Alternatively, you can make your child do impressions of leaves and flowers on a blank canvas. Let them dunk it in paint and slap it on the canvas, and watch them smile in delight!

106. Tree or Rock Painting

Why limit your toddler's creativity to a piece of blank paper? Take them back to the Stone Age and let their art bloom on the bark of a tree or a large rock. Keep those crayons and brushes aside. All they need is paint and their hands. The existing textures or colors on the tree or rock will add to their imagination, boosting their creativity.

107. Garden Assistant

Kids often mimic what their parents do. If you take your child along while tending to your lawn, they will likely mimic what you do. For instance, after watching you pull out weeds a few times, they will eventually start tugging on the grass themselves. They probably won't have enough strength to pull it out yet, but it's the act that matters. It shows that they are excited to assist you in your gardening chores. So the next time around, give them the tools for the job, like a toy watering can.

108. Dancing in the Rain

Back in the day, your parents may have warned you about playing in the rain. But you may have gone ahead and jumped and splashed around anyway; it was a lot of fun, wasn't it? Let your child experience that fun, too. Recent studies have shown that the benefits of playing in the rain far outweigh its drawbacks. Your child develops gross motor skills, thus learning how to be careful in wet weather at a very young age. Other benefits include increased immunity, peaked sensory skills, and improved physical skills.

109. Feeding Birds

Birds are nature's gift to humankind. But it's hard for children to watch birds up close. Their restlessness and quick movements often drive the birds away. Teach your little one how to make the birds come to them. Teach them how to feed those feathered creatures. They are generally hungry for sunflower seeds. Keep a bowl of it in your yard, and let your child watch as the birds flock together for a feast.

110. Walking Barefoot on Grass

It's best to let your child roam around in nature barefoot. It is probably the easiest kind of sensory play on this list. A few minutes of barefoot walking will start building the muscles of their feet, gradually enhancing their overall balance while walking or running. And, of course, the feel of grass, dirt, and pebbles will heighten their sense of touch.

111. Cloud/Star Gazing

Is your toddler tired of doing all the activities mentioned so far? Many of them can be exhausting. This is the perfect time to let them lie down on the cool turf and stare at passing clouds or the twinkling stars. Use your imagination to form different shapes with the clouds and describe your visualization to your child. Rock shapes are easiest to visualize, and their developing imagination can connect with the shapes they most recently played with.

Before you head out with your little one to explore nature, there are a few precautions you need to take. Make sure to clear the area of any rocks with jagged edges or pieces of glass. Scour the vicinity for bees or other harmful insects. Most importantly, don't let your child out of your sight, especially if you are in a public park.

Chapter 7: Having Fun in the Kitchen

You don't have to wait for your children to join school to start learning about science when you can easily do that at home. The kitchen is one of the best places you can teach your toddler about basic science. Even something as simple as melting chocolate can be a learning experience for your child and an opportunity for you to spend time with them. You can do various activities like cooking, baking, experimenting, or trying out sensory activities with your little one. The creative opportunities in a kitchen are endless, and the best thing about these activities is that you probably have all the supplies you need already in the kitchen.

Toddlers can learn about science in the kitchen.
https://www.pexels.com/photo/mother-and-child-in-the-kitchen-5082625/

In addition to science experiments, your child can partake in simple cooking rituals to help with their cognitive development. In fact, cooking is considered a STEM activity, and toddlers are completely capable of cooking with basic utensils, some simple appliances, and your supervision. These activities will save time, keep your child occupied, and help them learn basic concepts like following instructions, measuring, mixing, counting, etc. More than anything, children love to help you in the kitchen. Sure, they tend to make a mess, but with the right activities, it will be worth it.

Kitchen Experiments

112. Milk Swirl Experiment (Ages 3-11)

This simple science experiment is safe for children of all ages and super interesting, especially for toddlers. Plus, you'll find all the ingredients in your kitchen. The end result is a beautiful explosion of colors that leaves toddlers – and even you – in awe.

Materials:

- Food coloring
- Whole milk
- Dishwashing soap
- A plate or bowl
- A jar or cup
- A cotton swab

Instructions:

1. Gather all the materials and place them on the kitchen counter where your child can see them.
2. Have your child pour some milk into the plate or bowl.
3. Ask your child to pour one drop of each food coloring right into the center of the milk.
4. In a jar or cup, take some of the liquid dishwashing soap. Dip the cotton swab into the soap until the end is immersed.
5. Finally, give your child the cotton swab and ask them to touch it gently to the food coloring drops in the milk.
6. Enjoy the final explosion of colors!

113. Fizzing Colors (Ages 3-12)

This is another colorful kitchen experiment that is simple to execute and can catch your toddler's attention. Plus, you only need three simple ingredients for this experiment.

Materials:

- Food coloring
- 1 cup baking soda
- ½ cup white vinegar
- A baking sheet or pie pan
- An eye dropper or pipette

Instructions:

1. Gather your ingredients and arrange them on the kitchen counter.
2. Put an even layer of baking soda on the baking sheet or pie pan, covering the surface uniformly.
3. Hand your child the food coloring bottles and ask them to pour drops all over the baking soda. Make sure they don't squeeze out excessive quantities of the color solutions.
4. Take some of the white vinegar and drop it in using the eye dropper, pipette, or even a straw.

5. Voila! You'll see an explosion of colors full of bubbles.

114. Instant Sensory Snow (Ages 3-8)

If your toddler loves to play with snow, this activity is perfect for them. It creates instant snow for sensory play; although it's fake, the snow will feel real to them. The best part? All it takes is three simple steps.

Materials:

- ¼ cup White colored shampoo
- ½ cup Baking soda
- Measuring cup
- Tray

Instructions:

1. Cover the tray with the baking soda.
2. Add the shampoo to the top of the baking soda.
3. Ask your child to use their hands to mix these two ingredients together. After a while, the mixture will take on a less crumbly and sticky mixture and start to resemble the texture of real snow.

115. Sink or Float? (Ages 3-8)

This simple activity will teach your toddler about the concept of sink and float. This experiment is fun for children of every age but especially helpful for toddlers.

Materials:

- A large container for water
- Two containers
- Small toys

Instructions:

1. Ask your child to gather all their toys for a fun activity.
2. Label the two containers: "sink" and "float."
3. Fill up the large container with water.
4. Explain the concept of floating and sinking to your child, and then ask them to drop their toys into the water container one by one.
5. If the toy floats, put it into the float container. If it sinks, it goes into the other container.
6. Halfway through the activity, start making predictions about whether the toy will sink or float to make the activity more fun.

116. Marshmallow Slime (Ages 3-10)

Slime is all the rage among children of all ages. But instead of getting your child one of those toxic chemical slimes, what if you could make edible slime with marshmallows? Of course, this doesn't mean they should be encouraged to eat this, but only that it's safe for young children.

Materials:

- Food coloring
- Powdered sugar
- Measuring cups
- Bowl and spoon
- Marshmallow fluff

Instructions:

1. Transfer the marshmallow fluff to a bowl, and add the food coloring to the mix.
2. Next, place the powdered sugar on a clean surface and place the now-colored marshmallow fluff on top of it.
3. Knead the mixture until your desired consistency is achieved.

117. Edible Structures

This activity introduces the concepts of engineering and construction to children while combining yummy snacks in the process. It's very easy to set up and uses supplies already available in your kitchen.

Materials:

- Toothpicks
- Apple slices
- Marshmallows
- Cheese blocks (small)
- Crackers

Instructions:

1. Ask your child to build a structure using the toothpicks and the snacks by stabbing the toothpick into the snack.
2. You can create towers, tall structures, horizontal shapes, or any kind of geometric shape as long as the structure remains stable.
3. Tell your child they can have all the snacks they use to make their structure.

118. Grow Salt Crystals

This fun activity for growing salt crystals will keep your child's curiosity and attention for a while. It's a safe experiment that can be performed with a toddler and uses just a few simple ingredients.

Materials:

- Water
- Construction paper
- Salt
- Tray
- Container

- Pencil, scissors, and hole puncher
- A string

Instructions:

1. Cut a small shape from construction paper and punch a hole near the top.
2. Tie a string through the hole and hang the shape inside the container.
3. Pour water into the tray and place the container in the center.
4. Sprinkle salt evenly into the container.
5. Let it sit undisturbed in a warm area to allow crystals to form.
6. Check regularly, and remove the shape when crystals form.
7. Let the crystals dry completely.

119. Dancing Raisins

Is this science? Magic? This activity helps children learn about the states of matter, densities, and simple science. Sounds tough, right? It's actually easier than it sounds.

Materials:

- Glass
- Raisins
- Club soda

Instructions:

1. Pour the club soda into the glass until it's a quarter filled.
2. Ask your child to add some raisins to the glass.
3. Observe as the raisins go to the bottom of the glass, then float to the top and back to the bottom again, as science works its magic.

Tasty Recipes

120. Garden Salad

If you want to get your child to eat healthy, have them make a garden salad with you. They might not be interested in eating it if you make it, so ensure they're involved. Have them chop the lettuce and add the ingredients together.

Ingredients:

- 1 to 2 tbsp of ranch dressing
- 2 to 4 tbsp of diced cooked chicken
- 1 cup lettuce, sweet corn, diced tomatoes, diced cucumbers

Instructions:

1. In a large bowl, ask your child to add the ingredients one by one.
2. Once added, you can season the salad with salt, pepper, and ranch dressing.
3. Mix the salad with two spoons or forks, and have your child follow your lead.

121. Banana Bread

This toddler-friendly recipe is not only delicious but also easy to follow. Your toddler can even do all the steps themselves if you guide them through the process.

Ingredients:

- ½ plain flour
- 2 bananas
- 1 ½ self-rising flour
- ½ cup brown sugar
- ½ cup milk
- 2 eggs
- 50g of butter
- Cinnamon

Instructions:

1. Before you can start preparing the bread, preheat the oven to 180 degrees Celsius
2. Combine all of the ingredients in a large container and mix them thoroughly
3. Mash the bananas in a bowl, then add the butter, milk, and eggs.
4. Add this mixture to the large container, and then transfer it into a greased loaf pan
5. Put this in the oven for about 45 minutes until it's done.

122. Quesadillas

Quesadillas are the perfect snack! This easy recipe will help your toddler learn how to make simple quesadillas, and once they get the hang of it, you can add more ingredients to the basic recipe.

Ingredients:

- 4 tortillas - medium-sized
- 2 cups of shredded cheese (Mozzarella, Cheddar)
- Fillings - as desired (shredded chicken, green bell peppers, sliced onions, mushrooms, diced tomatoes, cilantro, spinach, sweet corn, etc.)

Instructions:

1. Coat a large pan or griddle with olive oil and heat it at medium-high for two minutes before adding the tortilla.
2. Let it warm for about 30 seconds, and then add cheese to one side of the tortilla.
3. Once the cheese is a little melted, add the rest of the ingredients, fold the tortilla, and press.
4. Before flipping the tortilla, cook for about five minutes and press using a spatula.

123. Quiche

This simple recipe is perfect for toddlers to learn about stirring and mixing food. You can have your child crack eggs and beat them to make this yummy veggie quiche.

Ingredients:

- 1 pie dough
- 3 to 4 slices of bacon
- 1 cup cheese (Swiss)
- 5 large eggs
- 1 ½ cups of mixed vegetables (bell peppers, yellow onion, mushrooms, broccoli)
- ½ tsp salt
- White pepper

Instructions:

1. Preheat the oven to 375 degrees. Roll out the dough into a pie plate and set it up. Place it into the fridge to cool.
2. Cook the bacon over medium heat until it browns. Once done, remove the bacon, but keep the pan on the stove.
3. Now, add the vegetables to the pan one by one and cook for a few minutes.
4. Whip up the eggs, salt, and pepper in a separate bowl.
5. Add the egg mixture, bacon, and vegetables to the pie plate, half at a time. Make two layers until the pan is filled up.
6. Place it into the oven and let it bake for 30 minutes.

124. Vegetable Soup

Vegetable soup is relatively easier to make than most food items and will teach your children how to measure the ingredients. Having them cut the veggies with a safe knife will also help develop their skills.

Ingredients:

- Salt and pepper
- Chopped spring onions
- Corn flour
- Sweet corn
- Chopped coriander leaves
- Milk

Instructions:

1. Cook the tender corn separately in a pressure cooker.
2. Blend the remaining corn with half of the milk and salt to create a smooth paste. Strain the mixture.
3. Transfer the mixture to a pan and cook on low heat. Add milk and coriander, then boil it on medium heat for five minutes.
4. Dissolve the corn flour in the remaining milk, mix well, and add it to the pan along with the seasoning.
5. Garnish with spring onions.

125. Sandwiches

Helping your child learn the basic skill of making a sandwich at an early age is a favor to both of you. All they have to do is gather the ingredients and place them on the bread. It doesn't even involve fire or a knife.

Ingredients:

- 1 large / 2 small slices of cooked chicken breast
- Lettuce
- Tomato
- 3 slices whole meal bread
- 1 tbsp hummus
- Cucumber
- Carrot

Instructions:

1. Toast the bread and cut off the crusts if you feel like it. Totally optional!
2. Grab a vegetable peeler and shred the cucumber and carrot into thin strips.
3. Slather some yummy hummus on all three slices of bread.
4. Take one slice and pile on the lettuce and juicy chicken breast.
5. Add another slice of bread and load it up with tomato, cucumber, and carrot.
6. Finally, pop that last slice of toasted bread on top, and you're good to go!

126. Grilled Cheese

This is every child's favorite meal. This simple recipe makes it the best choice for parents and children alike.

Ingredients:

- Bread
- Cheese
- Mashed Sweet Potato
- Butter

Instructions:

1. Take one piece of toast and spread the sweet potato on it. On another piece, add the cheese.
2. Melt some butter in a pan and then place the bread with the fillings facing up. Swirl it around a bit to coat the bread with butter. Cook until the undersides of both slices are nicely toasted.
3. Put the two slices of bread together and press down gently.
4. Cut it up, and it's ready to be served. Enjoy!

Participating in the kitchen doesn't just have to be an adult's job. Having your child help with cooking – and even the simple science experiments mentioned in this chapter – will help improve their cognitive development significantly. Plus, you'll get to spend time with your little one while doing your chores!

Chapter 8: Developing Cognition

During toddlerhood, children undergo an intense phase of cognitive development, allowing their minds to process and organize information more effectively. This encourages them to learn about their environment, improve their language acquisition skills, and develop avenues for self-expression. Consequently, the cognition-boosting activities geared toward toddlers must be engaging and adaptable to the children's individual needs and personalities.

This chapter delves into activities specifically designed to boost cognitive development in toddlers. These exercises aim to improve problem-solving abilities, memory, and logical thinking. On top of that, the different games and activities are not just educational but also fun, cultivating a positive attitude toward learning and thinking.

127. Memory Game with Flashcards

Using pairs of picture cards for a simple memory game will powerfully affect your child's cognitive development. Flashcard games improve concentration and memory skills. Start with simple shapes, colors, nature, and literary or math concepts like animals, letters, and numbers. Make it a daily practice to show them 1-2 flashcards (at first; later, you can increase the amount) and have them memorize the contents to stimulate their minds.

MEMORY GAME WITH FLASHCARDS

red	green	blue	orange

yellow	pink	gray	purple

red	green	blue	orange

yellow	pink	gray	purple

128. Close-Ended Games

Close-ended games foster children's cognitive development by promoting their problem-solving skills. Activities most recommended for close-ended learning involve pegs and peg boards, mazes, gears, and stacking rings. However, you can use any toys, activities, or items that encourage your child to be persistent in completing a task. No matter how hard they have worked to succeed, the sense of gratification they experience later builds up their confidence and motivates them to engage in new cognition-developing experiences.

Here's an example of a close-ended activity, stacking rings:

1. Get your toddler to sit on a mat and place the ring dowel in front of them.
2. First, slowly stack the rings yourself.
3. Start removing the rings one by one and examining them in front of your child.
4. Show that you can put your hand through the ring or look through it, and encourage the child to do the same.
5. Once they understand that the hole in the middle allows the rings to be stacked on the dowel, tell your child about the different sizes.
6. Explain that the rings can only be stacked in a specific order, which depends on their size.
7. Show this to your child by placing the largest ring on the dowel, followed by the next one in size. Finish up with the smallest ring.
8. Have them try stacking the rings by themselves. If they make a mistake, explain what this means. For example, if they try to put on the smallest ring first, they won't be able to do this because of its size.

129. Color Sorter Activities

Color sorters are great for teaching young toddlers about the fun world of colors. As your child explores the different colors, they become more and more interested in memorizing and recalling the colors of different objects around them. Buy or make a color sorter for your child to boost their logic and reasoning skills.

Here is how to make a DIY color sorter:

1. Get colored paper in 3-4 different colors and items to sort. For younger children, these should be small toys (preferably uniform ones that come in different colors).
2. Tape the papers onto the ground and put down a handful of toys.
3. Ask your child to sort the toys by color.
4. If needed, offer suggestions like, "You need to match the toy with the paper." or "The red toy goes on top of the red paper, the yellow to the yellow paper..."

130. Learning about Cause and Effect

Toys with buttons to push are great for teaching your toddler about cause and effect. Understanding this phenomenon is fundamental for healthy cognitive development in children. It can be as simple as using a toy that makes a sound or lights up when your child pushes a button. They will have tons of fun and learn that every action has an effect.

131. Stacking Wooden Blocks

Stacking wooden blocks is probably one of the most well-tried activities for enhancing cognitive development in young children. It's relatively simple, and you'll only need wooden blocks of various sizes and colors. Encourage them to stack the toys any way they want to foster creativity. As they do, they use their imagination, develop logic and memory skills, and more. If needed, offer some suggestions for making a particular shape.

132. Exploring Textures through Touch and Feel

Your toddler probably has tons of toys with different shapes and materials. So why not put random toys in a box for a texture exploration activity? They will enjoy sorting through them and hone plenty of cognitive functions in the process. Like in many other facets of children's development, sensory activities like touching and exploring different textures play an enormous role in cognitive development. You can incorporate this exercise into activities like playing outdoors, exploring nature, or getting familiar with arts and crafts. For example, letting your child explore the different textures of playdough and other craft materials will encourage them to consider how to use them. They learn how the different materials feel separately and together to decide whether it's a good idea to combine them or not. If you have an older toddler, let them decide what items they want to explore - but make sure they're age-appropriate and don't represent a choking hazard.

133. Hiding Objects

Finding hidden objects makes children use several cognitive processes, including logic, reasoning, and visual and short-term memory.

Instructions:

1. Show your toddler a small toy (something you can hide between your palms) and ask them to take a good look at it.
2. Then, ask them to look away and close your hands over the toy.
3. Lastly, ask your toddler what toys are between your hands.
4. Once your child has mastered the previous step, you can step it up by hiding objects under a blanket or towel. Make sure it's an item they're familiar with.
5. Have them look for the object. They'll have to recall what the items look like as they can't see it directly.
6. You can then start hiding objects in other easily accessible places to foster your child's desire for exploration and discovery. Both of these are fundamental for cognitive development.

134. Setting Up Simple Daily Routines

Setting up simple yet consistent routines for your child isn't only beneficial for laying a foundation for the scheduled activities they'll be required to partake in once they start kindergarten and school, but it's also great for enhancing their cognitive abilities like logic and reasoning. Learning about routines encourages children to develop the ability to follow instructions. From ages two and up, toddlers can understand when it's time to eat, get dressed, take a bath, tell stories, go to a park, and play. If these activities come in a sequence, they'll always know what comes next and learn to expect it. Routines foster a sense of discipline and normalcy, which contributes to balanced development. The best way to get your child to adhere to routines is to give them choices while teaching the specific task-time relation. For example, before snack time, let them choose between two options. Or, let them choose which toy they want to play with during bath time. Nurturing their drive for independence is just as crucial for your toddler's cognitive development as is adherence to routines.

135. Sorting-Based Toys and Games

Older toddlers can identify toys and small household objects and sort them. You can Create a homemade shape sorter with a cardboard box and colored shapes to get your toddler to recognize and categorize different shapes. You can start by asking them to sort blocks or toys based on color, shape, or size. Then, you can incorporate sorting games into their schedule, like meal or bath time. For example, you can give your toddlers different measuring cups and let them play with them in the bathtub. Then, ask them to use the largest one to scoop water over a bath toy. They will have to figure out which one they should use. 2-3-year-olds can be asked to help sort household items.

136. Encourage Letter and Number Learning

Letters and numbers are the basic tenets for learning pre-literacy language and math skills, so it's a good idea to familiarize your child with these as early as they can grasp this concept. There are numerous ways to teach toddlers numbers and letters - from teaching counting and alphabet songs to encouraging them to use magnets and blocks depicting letters and numbers. For older toddlers acquainted with the names of household items, you can cut out letters and stick them to the objects whose names begin with that letter. Look for opportunities to count objects with your toddler whenever possible throughout the day.

137. Organizing and Recognizing Toys and Household Objects

Toddlers can learn a lot from classifying objects. For younger toddlers, focus on teaching them how to organize toys and other objects by shape and color. Once they've mastered this, you can ask them to arrange colored blocks, pegs, and other items from large to small. The next step is to encourage them to pick out items of a specific color or shape. Then, take it a step further and ask your toddler to pick out other household items (like the smallest cup, a blanket of a specific color, etc.) as you go with them about their daily routines.

138. Age-Appropriate Puzzles

Introducing simple jigsaw puzzles to encourage problem-solving skills and persistence is a great way to improve your child's logic and reasoning skills. Age-appropriate puzzles for toddlers come in all shapes and sizes - from interactive animal puzzles to 2D or 3D puzzles for spatial play. The latter usually has smaller pieces the child needs to fit together to create a larger object. During this, they learn how to work out how the smaller pieces can come together in space through trial and error. Likewise, interactive animal puzzles require children to match the sounds of the animals with their pictures. Whichever type of puzzle you get, make sure to start with a small number of pieces. For younger toddlers (12-18 months), this is around 2-4 pieces, while older children (20 months and older) can match up to 10 pieces. Your child must be able to visually identify the parts so they can use their logic and memory to complete the puzzle.

Here is a quick guide for helping your toddler master puzzles (if they haven't already):

1. Put the puzzle piece in front of your toddler and encourage them to put the pieces together.
2. Let them lead by letting them figure out the logical orientation of the different pieces. It will make them more interested in the activity - and, consequently, learn more.

3. Following your child's lead, you'll learn about their interest and provide further tools for their cognitive development. You'll also be able to notice if they get stuck in finding the specific position of the puzzle pieces.

4. If your child has difficulty with this activity, ask them to think about how to solve the problem (for ages 2 and up) or offer solutions (for 1-2-year-olds). For example, you can ask them to look closer and determine where else a specific piece fits or suggest that they turn it the other way.

5. When your toddler gets it right and completes the puzzle, praise them for their effort to boost their confidence and encourage them to tackle new problems.

139. Gathering Objects

Gathering objects is an open-ended activity that encourages children to explore and manipulate the world around them. Through it, your child can learn all about the items they explore and acquire new skills. For example, while gathering objects, they'll see that different items can be used in multiple ways. Likewise, they become more persistent in finding specific things and can even learn simple math and science concepts. They develop their reasoning skills and learn by example as they interact with you or whoever is helping them gather the object.

To encourage this cognition-boosting opportunity, make a list of objects you want your toddler to find, then have them explore, collect, manipulate, and experiment with the items. Some ideas for gathering items are muffin pans, cups, funnels, small bottles or jugs, plastic utensils and lids, small mirrors, pieces of fabric, tubes, and other household items.

140. DIY Toddler Puzzles

Helping your toddler create their own puzzle improves cognitive development. You can help them make simple but interactive puzzles - or, if they have an older sibling to help them, even better. Either way, it can be a wonderful bonding activity for children and parents.

Instructions:

1. Have your child paint or draw a picture - or you or an older sibling can do this instead if your toddler is too little for this.

2. Cut the picture into four or more pieces (depending on the child's age - the younger they are, the fewer pieces they can match).

3. Encourage your child to put the picture back together by arranging the "puzzle" pieces in the appropriate order and placement. This will make them use and develop their problem-solving skills.

141. Matching Post-It Shapes

Matching Post-its is another marvelous way to introduce toddlers to shapes, colors, numbers, letters, and other concepts. If you don't have a ready-made activity on hand, you can always make one from Post-it notes. Here is how to do it:

1. Get sticky notes in different colors. Cut little shapes like squares, hearts, circles, rectangles, and triangles from each color. Keep the stick part when cutting.

2. Cut the exact shapes you made from sticky notes from colored cardstock, just a little bigger.

3. Place double-sided tape on the wall or table and attach the cardstock cutouts.

4. Arrange the small shapes under them and have your child match the sticky shapes to the corresponding bigger ones by attaching them to the right place.

5. You can coordinate colors, too, depending on your toddler's abilities.

6. Encourage your child to choose the corresponding shapes themselves, but step in to help if they are stuck.

Chapter 9: Fostering Social Strength

Social development is vital in shaping children's abilities to interact, communicate, and collaborate effectively with others. Engaging in activities that enhance interaction, sharing, empathy, and cooperative play can be an excellent way to promote these essential social skills while making learning enjoyable and engaging.

Promoting social skills is important for toddlers.

Enhancing Interaction

One key element of social development is encouraging interaction capabilities in your child. Promoting your children to engage in conversations, educating them on the benefits of active listening, and letting them understand the necessity of non-verbal communication will let them create stronger social connections. Interactive activities like team-building exercises, group discussions, and collaborative projects can help children boost their communication skills. These activities will also foster a sense of mutual understanding and let them build better connections with their peers.

Promoting Sharing

Making your child understand the necessity of sharing is an awesome social strength to develop. The focus of sharing here is to share beyond material possessions, like sharing experiences, ideas, and emotions. Encouraging your child to share their interests, thoughts, and ideas promotes a sense of being connected. Community service projects, group storytelling events, and team exercises are excellent platforms to let your child share their perspective and stay motivated through the supportive and collaborative environment.

Developing Empathy

Empathy is one of the foundation pillars of social strength, which enables the child to understand and respect the feelings of others. When your child develops empathy, it promotes the development of healthy relationships with their peers, allows them to resolve conflicts, and helps them understand how to adequately address the people around them while respecting their emotional state. These activities help children better understand diverse perspectives, cultivate compassion, and strengthen their emotional intelligence, ultimately nurturing their ability to connect with others on a deeper level.

Encouraging Cooperative Play

Co-op play encourages your child to work together with other children toward achieving a common goal. The activity promotes problem-solving skills, letting your child understand teamwork and cooperation. Cooperative games, group challenges, and related projects should be encouraged in your child as those allow them to experience sharing, the necessity of communication, and to develop better negotiation skills. Co-op play will also let your child understand the significance of pursuing a common goal over individual success and recognize the value of teamwork in certain situations. They will eventually develop strong social bonds with their peers.

As parents, fostering social strength in children is crucial for their overall development and future success. Engaging children in play activities that promote interaction, sharing, empathy, and cooperative play helps them develop essential social skills and makes the learning process enjoyable and engaging. By providing opportunities for children to interact, share, empathize, and collaborate, you empower them to navigate the complexities of the modern world, build strong relationships, and become confident and empathetic individuals.

Fostering Social Strength through Play Activities

142. Turn-Taking Games:

Instructions:

1. Gather children and introduce them to turn-based games like "Pass the Ball" or "Duck Duck Goose."
2. Give the ball to a child and instruct them to pass it to the child on their right.
3. Encourage them to wait patiently for their turn and let the ball be passed down to them.

In "Duck Duck Goose," children sit in a circle, and one child goes around tapping others on the head, saying "duck." When they say "goose," the tapped child gets up and chases the first child around the circle, trying to tag them before they reach the vacant spot.

Duck Duck Goose.
Jon Fleshman, CC BY 2.0 DEED <https://creativecommons.org/licenses/by/2.0/>
https://flickr.com/photos/louisvilleusace/5740729000/

Benefits:

Turn-taking games promote sharing, patience, and cooperation. Children learn to wait for their turn, respect others' opportunities, and practice social skills in a playful environment.

143. Puppet Show:

Instructions:

1. Provide children with finger puppets and encourage them to create a puppet show.
2. You can provide a scenario the children can enact, letting their imaginations run wild.
3. Now, encourage each child to express their feelings and participate in the puppet show.
4. Instruct the children to take turns, switch finger puppets with other children, and interact with each other through these finger puppets.

PUPPET SHOW

Benefits:

Enacting a puppet show fosters social strength by developing better communication skills and letting children express their opinions, emotions, and creativity through storytelling.

144. Building Blocks:

Instructions:

1. Provide building blocks or construction toys to the children.
2. Encourage them to work together to build structures.
3. Children can take turns adding blocks, sharing ideas, and collaborating on building different structures like towers, houses, or bridges.

Benefits:

This activity promotes collaboration, teamwork, and creativity in your children as they understand the benefits of working together, respecting the opinions of others, and learning to work together on a common goal while sharing the available resources.

Building blocks encourage creativity
https://pxhere.com/en/photo/499153

145. Arts and Crafts:

Instructions:

1. Gather art supplies like crayons, markers, chart papers, scissors, and related tools.
2. Introduce children to the art station, explaining about the activity.
3. They can pick the desired art supplies and craft the art projects they like.

4. Instruct the children to collaborate, share their art supplies with other children, and create a collaborative art project.

Benefits:

Collaborative art projects foster cooperation, communication, and creativity. Children learn to share materials, negotiate ideas, and appreciate each other's contributions.

146. Role-Playing:

Instructions:

1. Provide costumes or props, or encourage children to use their imagination to act out different roles.
2. They can pretend to be characters like doctors, teachers, or animals and engage in imaginative play scenarios.
3. Have them take turns playing different roles and interacting with each other.

Benefits:

Role-playing activities enhance social skills, empathy, and creative thinking. Children learn to understand different perspectives, practice communication, and develop cooperation through collaborative play.

147. Storytelling:

Instructions:

1. Provide picture books or story cards with illustrations.
2. Children can take turns telling stories based on the pictures or cards provided.
3. Encourage them to use their imagination and create a story together, each contributing to different parts or taking turns adding elements to the narrative.

Benefits:

Storytelling activities promote listening skills, turn-taking, and imagination. Children develop language skills, creativity, and cooperative storytelling abilities.

148. Cooperative Board Games:

Instructions:

1. Choose cooperative board games such as Snakes and Ladders or Pandemic.
2. Gather children around the game board and explain the rules.
3. Emphasize that the goal is to work together as a team to achieve a common objective.
4. Encourage them to discuss strategies, make joint decisions, and take turns playing the game.

Benefits:

Cooperative board games foster teamwork, problem-solving, and sharing. Children learn to collaborate, communicate, and support each other while enjoying the game.

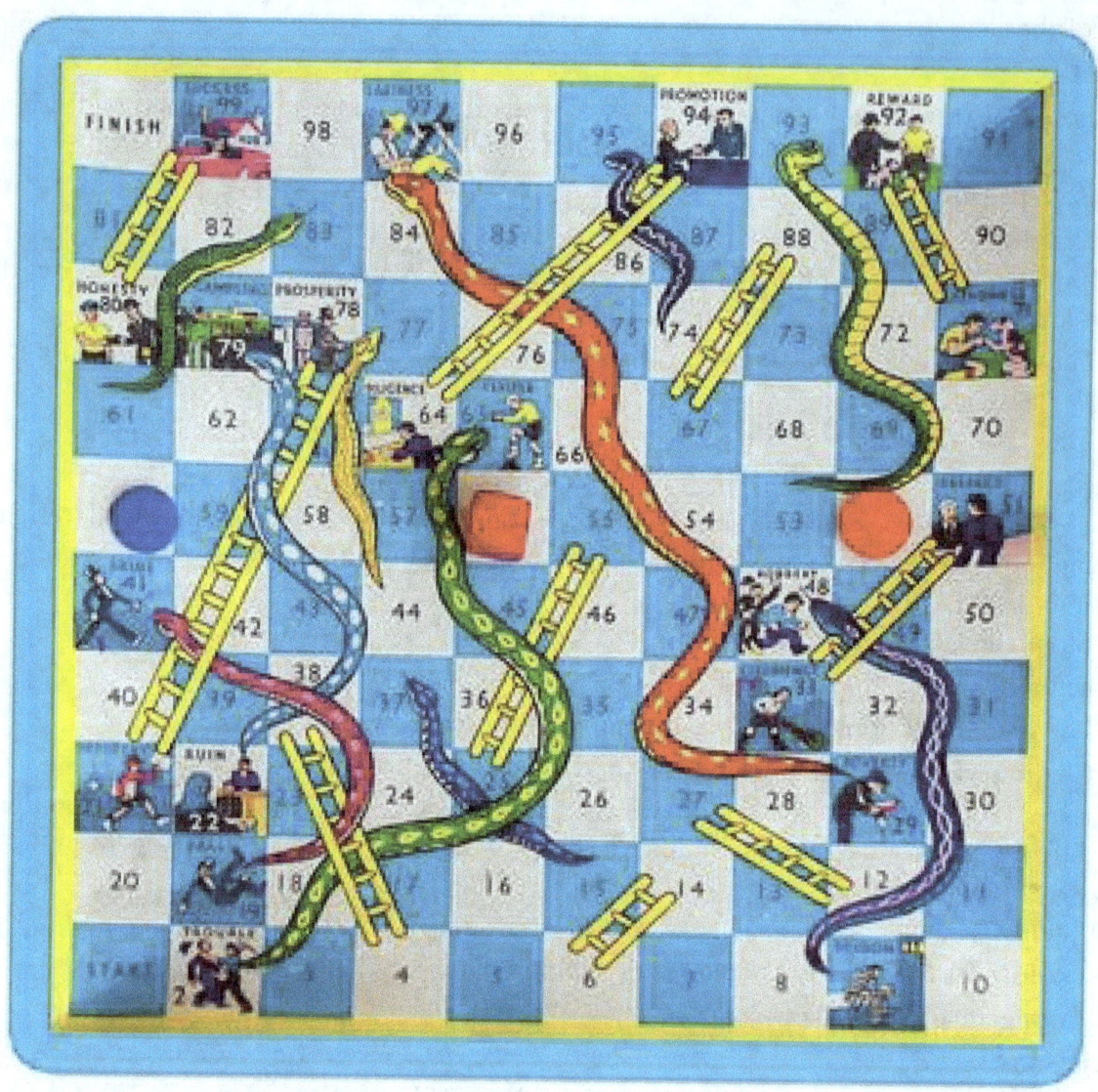

Snakes and Ladders is a fun cooperative board game for children and adults.

149. Outdoor Scavenger Hunt:

Instructions:

1. Create a scavenger hunt list with specific items for children to find in nature or their surroundings.

2. Divide children into teams or pairs and provide them with bags or baskets to collect the items.

3. Encourage them to work together, communicate, and help each other find the items on the list.

Benefits:

Outdoor scavenger hunts promote cooperation, communication, and observation skills. Children learn to collaborate, share responsibilities, and appreciate the value of teamwork.

150. Group Art Project:

Instructions:

1. Provide a large canvas or poster board and art supplies.
2. Children can collaboratively create a large artwork by taking turns adding their own touches.
3. Encourage them to discuss ideas, share materials, and work together to complete the artwork.

Benefits:

Group art projects encourage teamwork, communication, and creativity. Children learn to respect others' ideas, share resources, and contribute to a shared artistic vision.

151. Cooking or Baking Together:

Instructions:

1. Choose a simple recipe and involve children in preparing it.
2. Provide them with age-appropriate tasks and utensils.
3. Encourage them to take turns measuring ingredients, stirring, or decorating.
4. Emphasize the importance of cooperation, following instructions, and sharing responsibilities.

Benefits:

Cooking or baking together promotes cooperation, following instructions, and sharing. Children learn to work together, practice basic culinary skills, and enjoy the fruits of their collective efforts.

152. Musical Jam Session:

Instructions:

1. Gather a variety of musical instruments, real or makeshift, and invite children to participate in a music jam session.
2. Encourage them to take turns playing instruments, singing, or creating rhythms together. Promote communication, cooperation, and respect for each other's contributions.

Benefits:

Musical jam sessions foster creativity, cooperation, and turn-taking. Children learn to listen, communicate, and collaborate while expressing themselves through music.

153. Sensory Play:

Instructions:

1. Set up a sensory play station with materials like sand, water, or playdough.
2. Encourage children to explore and play together, taking turns and sharing sensory experiences.
3. Provide tools and molds for them to use and engage in cooperative sensory play.

Benefits:

Sensory play activities promote cooperation, sharing, and sensory development. Children learn to communicate, negotiate, and engage in collaborative sensory experiences.

154. Building a Fort:

Instructions:

1. Provide blankets, pillows, and chairs to create a fort or a cozy reading nook.
2. Encourage children to work together, plan the structure, and construct the fort.
3. They can take turns arranging the materials, suggesting ideas, and creating a comfortable space to enjoy.

Benefits:

Building forts promotes teamwork, problem-solving, and imaginative play. Children learn to cooperate, communicate, and collaborate in creating a shared space.

155. Group Dance or Movement Activity:

Instructions:

1. Play upbeat music and encourage children to dance or engage in movement activities together.
2. Promote group dances or simple choreographed movements that require coordination and cooperation.
3. Encourage them to take turns leading or suggesting dance moves.

Benefits:

Group dance or movement activities foster coordination, cooperation, and self-expression. Children learn to follow instructions, cooperate with others, and express themselves creatively.

156. Cooperative Sports:

Instructions:

1. Choose cooperative sports games such as relay races or group challenges.
2. Divide children into teams and explain the rules.
3. Encourage them to work together, communicate, and support each other to achieve the common goal.
4. Emphasize the importance of taking turns, sharing responsibilities, and celebrating collective achievements.

Benefits:

Cooperative sports activities promote teamwork, communication, and physical coordination. Children learn to collaborate, strategize, and appreciate the value of collective effort in sportsmanship.

Fostering teamwork within toddlers and developing social and interpersonal skills are necessary for their overall growth and development. By engaging in activities that promote collaboration and cooperation, toddlers learn valuable skills that lay the foundation for their social interactions and relationships later in life.

Teamwork encourages toddlers to work together towards a common goal, whether building a block tower, completing a puzzle, or participating in a group activity. Through these experiences, they understand the importance of sharing responsibilities, coordinating efforts, and relying on others. By working as a team, toddlers learn to communicate effectively, listen to others' ideas, and respect diverse perspectives.

Developing social and interpersonal skills is essential for toddlers to navigate social situations and build positive relationships. By engaging in collaborative activities, toddlers learn how to take turns, share resources, and resolve conflicts peacefully. They develop empathy and learn to understand and respect the emotions and feelings of others. These skills help them to interact with their peers in a considerate and inclusive manner, fostering harmonious social dynamics and reducing instances of conflict.

Teamwork and social interaction also contribute to developing important cognitive and emotional skills. Toddlers learn problem-solving abilities as they negotiate and find solutions collectively. They develop patience as they learn to wait for their turn and understand that everyone's contributions are valuable. Through collaborative play, they gain a sense of belonging, self-confidence, and a positive self-image as they realize that their ideas and efforts matter within the group.

Furthermore, teamwork and social development provide a solid foundation for future academic success. By learning to work effectively in groups, toddlers develop skills such as active listening, cooperation, and effective communication that are vital for collaborative learning environments. These skills will continue to benefit them as they progress through school, higher education, and later in their careers.

Fostering teamwork within toddlers and developing their social and interpersonal skills are crucial aspects of their overall development. By engaging in collaborative activities, toddlers learn the value of working together, communicating effectively, and respecting others. These skills provide a strong foundation for building positive relationships, navigating social situations, and succeeding academically and professionally later in life.

Chapter 10: Quiet Time and Its Endless Possibilities

Quiet time is an essential part of the day for toddlers, as it gives them a chance to take a break from some of the more stimulating activities of the day and relax for a while. This part of the day involves them playing quietly and on their own, so it also gives parents some time away from the toddlers. This alone time proves to be quite nurturing for young children, as it helps them become more independent, relaxed, and confident. When done daily, this part of the day reduces the frequency of your child's tantrums and meltdowns. Plus, you don't need hundreds of toys to make quiet time fun for your children. And don't even think about handing them a screen. All you need are open-ended activities that allow your child to use their creativity and imagination but are also low-key enough that they do not require supervision. This chapter includes several fun activities that you can include in your toddler's quiet time.

157. Coloring Activities

Coloring has a certain appeal to children, especially young toddlers. The activity of coloring can reduce stress and promote relaxation in children and even adults! It can also help with the development of their fine motor skills.

Materials:

- Colors
- Markers
- Crayons
- Coloring book
- Coloring pages
- Blank pages

Instructions:

1. You can either get your toddler a simple coloring book or print some coloring pages for them.
2. Alternatively, you can give them blank sheets to draw and color on.
3. Show them how to hold a colored pencil, marker, or crayon and how the color should be filled in.
4. Try not to limit their creativity by having them draw or color a specific way, and just let them do their own thing.

158. Building Toys

Building toys are among the most common activities children are engaged in during quiet time. Whether you get them large building blocks or tiny Lego sets, they will stay creatively engaged in the process while their fine motor abilities develop.

Materials:

- Building blocks or Lego sets
- Clean and safe play area

Instructions:

1. Set up a clean and safe play area.
2. Choose age-appropriate building blocks or Lego sets.
3. Show your toddler how to stack blocks or connect Lego pieces.
4. Let them use their creativity to build their own structures.
5. Offer guidance and support as needed.
6. Allow free playtime.
7. Clean up together after playtime.

159. Puzzles

Puzzles are interesting to children.
https://www.pexels.com/photo/assemble-challenge-combine-creativity-269399/

Puzzles are intriguing for young children, especially once you show them how they're done. To keep them engaged, you'll have to make sure the puzzle sets you get are neither too difficult nor too easy. Getting puzzles with colored pieces will be an added bonus to catch your child's attention. It's best to start with big, chunky pieces and then work your way to more complex ones.

Materials:
- Puzzles
- Play area

Instructions:
1. Show your child how to solve a simple puzzle to help them understand the process.
2. Encourage your child to observe the patterns and colors on the puzzle pieces.
3. Guide them in placing the pieces in their correct positions, only offering assistance when needed.
4. Support their problem-solving skills and celebrate each time they're successful.
5. Allow your child to work on the puzzles independently, and be there just in case they need help.
6. If you're using a puzzle with small pieces, you must watch your child closely to ensure they don't swallow a piece.

160. Pretend Play

Pretend play is something all children love to do. Their imagination works wonders for them, and they get to spend time alone. Whether your toddler likes to play doctor, house, or any other pretend scenario, all you need to do is give them the right props and some directions.

Materials:

- Play props and costumes
- Pretend play sets or accessories (e.g., kitchen set)
- Decorative elements (e.g., mini-furniture)
- Open-ended props (e.g., a blanket to make a fort)
- Printed or handmade visual aids (e.g., pretend money)

Instructions:

1. Ask your toddler what they would like to play with today. They'll probably have a favorite, like a teacher, doctor, or chef.
2. Gather the props, toys, or costumes they can use in their chosen scenario. For instance, if they want to play a doctor, get them their toy doctor set.
3. Set up a play area in their room where they can freely engage in this activity.
4. Let your child take the lead and start the scenario. Don't try to restrict their imagination by telling them to be rational.
5. Participate in the pretend play by taking on supporting roles, like being the patient in their doctor scenario.

161. Audiobooks

If you don't want your children to spend time looking at a screen, another way to keep them engaged and entertained is to put on audiobooks. There are numerous stories with engaging audiobooks that spark creativity and will be very interesting for your little one. This will also help with their literacy development, and they can learn valuable lessons along the way.

Materials:

- Audiobooks or audio story recordings
- Device or audio player
- Comfortable listening area or headphones

Instructions:

1. Choose stories that are age-appropriate for your child. For toddlers, some great books to start with are:
   - "Goodnight Moon" by Margaret Wise Brown
   - "The Very Hungry Caterpillar" by Eric Carle
   - "Brown Bear, Brown Bear, What Do You See?" by Bill Martin Jr. and Eric Carle
   - "Guess How Much I Love You" by Sam McBratney
   - "Where the Wild Things Are" by Maurice Sendak
   - "Corduroy" by Don Freeman

o "Dear Zoo" by Rod Campbell

o "The Cat in the Hat" by Dr. Seuss

2. Ask your child which story they want to listen to, and play the audio at a suitable volume.

3. Encourage your child to listen actively and let their imagination run wild.

4. After the story, ask your child about the lessons they learned.

162. Dry-Erase Activity Board

Get a whiteboard, also known as a dry-erase activity board, for your toddler to keep them engaged during quiet time. This will also help their educational learning, as they can practice their numbers and letters on it. They can even use colorful markers to make illustrations without making a mess of things.

Materials:

- Dry-Erase Activity Board (with built-in markers and erasers or separate markers and erasers)

- Dry-erase markers (non-toxic and washable)

- Soft cloth or tissue for erasing

Instructions:

1. Introduce the board and markers to your child, and explain how they can use them.

2. You can start by having them trace letters, numbers, shapes, or drawings to help their hand get steady.

3. Encourage them to be creative and explore different colors and drawings.

4. Make sure they don't try to ingest the markers or write on the walls when you're not looking.

163. Button Trees

This fun quiet time activity is an engaging task that will offer your child lots of learning opportunities. You'll have to create a colorful tree using pipe cleaners, and your child can thread buttons onto the tree branches. This will improve their creativity and enhance their hand-to-eye coordination.

Materials:

- Pipe cleaners in various colors

- Buttons in different sizes and colors

- Small container

Instructions:

1. Take a pipe cleaner of your chosen color and fold it in half to create the tree trunk.

2. Twist the folded end of the pipe cleaner a few times to secure the trunk shape.

3. Bend the rest of the pipe cleaner to form branches, leaving some space at the end for attaching buttons.

4. Ask your child to thread buttons into each branch one at a time.

5. You can ask them to first thread buttons of a specific color or size, then follow with the rest.

6. Have them count the buttons as they thread them into the tree branches.

7. Ensure you keep an eye on your child while playing with the buttons to prevent them from ingesting one.

164. Crazy Straws

For this fun, quiet time activity, you'll first have to craft the crazy straws sequence and then have your child play with the different shapes, colors, and sizes. You can have them sort colors, sizes, and shapes or even create a rainbow!

Materials:

- A few crazy straws
- Felt in different colors

Instructions:

1. Cut different shapes out of the felt. You can do circles, squares, triangles, hearts, and stars.
2. Punch a hole in the center of these shapes, big enough to fit the end of a straw.
3. Mix the shapes together and place them in a container. Place the straws on a surface, and ask your child to thread each shape into the crazy straws one by one.
4. Either instruct them to make a specific pattern or have them do it themselves.

165. Chalkboard Table

Reuse an old table and blackboard to make the perfect drawing space for your toddler. This may sound complicated, but you need to follow just a few steps to make one. Your child will love playing with different colored chalks and being able to scribble on a table.

Materials:

- An old table
- Paint roller
- Chalkboard paint
- Chalks

Instructions:

1. Clean the surface of the table you're using, and start painting the top with blackboard paint.
2. If you don't have a paint roller, you can always use a paintbrush, but remember it will take longer. Let the table dry.
3. After a few hours, paint a second coat over the dried paint and leave it to dry overnight.
4. Once it's done, test the surface by rubbing the side of the chalk onto the surface and rubbing it off with a board rubber.
5. Give your child some toddler and let them get creative.

166. Matching Objects

These simple toddler puzzles need little to no crafting or preparation and will keep your child engaged for a while.

Materials:

- Markers
- Cardstock
- Toys

- Scissors

Instructions:

1. Cut the cardstock in half.
2. Use the markers to trace your child's toys onto the cardstock. You can have your child choose their favorite toys and trace those yourself.
3. If your child knows how to trace, ask them to trace their toys themselves.
4. Now, mix up the toys, lay out the puzzle pieces, and have your toddler match each toy with its outline.

167. Calm Down Jar

Calm-down jars are a must-have if you have toddlers, especially if it's hard to get them to quiet down. These are also called mindfulness jars because their beautiful and glittering swirling patterns keep your child's attention.

Materials:

- Plastic bottles or jars
- Hot water
- Mixing bowl
- Whisk
- Liquid watercolor or food coloring
- Fine glitter
- Glue

Instructions:

1. Put some hot water in the mixing bowl, and add the clear glue to it. Mix thoroughly.
2. Add the watercolor, food color, and glitter into the mix, and whisk it again.
3. Once everything is blended completely, pour the mixture into the plastic bottle.
4. Mix one last time before transferring the mixture into the bottle to avoid leaving any glitter behind.
5. Shake the bottle vigorously and hand it to your child.

168. Action Figures and Dolls

Playing with action figures and dolls is a wonderful opportunity for children to engage in imaginative and creative play. With a collection of action figures or dolls and related accessories, toddlers bring their characters to life, create stories, and embark on exciting adventures.

Materials:

- Action figures or dolls
- Accessories or props

Instructions:

1. Gather action figures or dolls along with their accessories.
2. Encourage your child to create stories and scenarios with the figures/dolls.

3. Provide a designated play area or playmat for their playtime.
4. Let them dress up the figures/dolls and set up props for different scenes.

169. Latch Board

A latch board is a fun activity that aims to improve young children's fine motor abilities. It has all sorts of latches, hooks, locks, and keys. Playing with a latch board will keep your toddler engaged during quiet time, and this activity doesn't require you to supervise them.

Materials:

- Latch board (pre-made or DIY)
- Clean and safe play area

Instructions:

1. Get a latch board of appropriate difficulty for your child. This activity's purpose is to teach your toddler independence.
2. Introduce the board to your child and show them how to use the different hooks, keys, and latches.
3. Encourage your toddler to explore the latch board independently, allowing them to manipulate the latches and learn how they work.
4. Let them practice their fine motor skills by opening and closing the different mechanisms on the board.

170. Feed the Monster Game

This fun game is a fine motor skills development activity that can keep your child engaged. You'll have to turn an old empty tub of wipes into a monster and use pom poms, buttons, and other small items as food.

Materials:

- Empty box of wipes
- Craft supplies (construction paper, googly eyes, markers, glue)
- Pom poms, buttons, or other small items as "food"

Instructions:

1. Turn the empty box of wipes into a monster face using construction paper, googly eyes, markers, and glue.
2. Cut a mouth shape large enough to put small items in.
3. Scatter pom poms, buttons, or small items around the tub as "food."
4. Encourage your child to pick up the small items and feed them into the monster's mouth.
5. Support their fine motor skills and hand-eye coordination during play.
6. Celebrate each successful "feeding" and offer rewards or points.

171. Calming Yoga

Yoga can help your child wind down.
https://www.pexels.com/photo/cheerful-asian-mother-and-daughter-stretching-body-in-living-room-5094673/

Calming yoga is the perfect quiet-time activity if your little one has a hard time winding down for a nap. This activity provides a constructive outlet for all their unused energy and makes them tired enough to go to sleep. So, teach your child some basic yoga poses and practice them with your child at the end of their quiet time activities. You can even give them some simple yoga cards with visual cues to practice all the poses on their own.

Conclusion

Toddlers experience a better sense of self-confidence when they can put their creativity to use. They feel great when they realize they can create something with minimal assistance. They also feel proud of themselves when they receive positive feedback and reactions to something they've created. Showing a child that their artwork is valued will encourage them to continue working on their skills.

Children are met with various choices and conflicting ideas when they explore their creativity and spontaneous thoughts. Having to choose between certain color or pattern combinations, images to draw or color, and materials to use encourages them to make decisions and solve problems. Creative activities allow children to think outside the box and trust their judgment. Having fun is also important for a child's well-being, as it offers a break from routines, rules, and expectations. Creative activities offer a safe space for children where experimentation, mistakes, and expression are encouraged.

Now that you've read this book, you know how to channel your child's creativity into fruitful experiences. You know the go-to activities to do with your child whenever they need to work on their cognitive, sensory, physical, emotional, or social skills. The majority of a child's education happens at home. That's mainly because they have more space and freedom of expression there. Unfortunately, traditional educational systems suppress children's imaginative and creative tendencies. They turn down alternative ways of thinking and solving problems. The activities offered in this book will allow you to make the most of your child's time at home, ensuring healthy and enriching brain development.

Your home activities can bring your attention to their hidden talents and hobbies. Your child will never know if they like cooking, gardening, or beading if they never try it. This book might be why you discover your child is a skilled actor or singer. Applying the information you learned here will teach you a lot about yourself and your child.

Parents, caregivers, and babysitters can benefit from the activities in this book. Besides connecting and spending quality time with the toddler, creative play aids neural connectivity in the brain's frontal lobe during adolescence and early adulthood. The part of the brain that develops last is responsible for planning, sound decision-making, and prioritizing. Having fun with a toddler also allows you to get in touch with your inner child and unwind from the responsibilities and stressors of everyday life.

Check out another book in the series

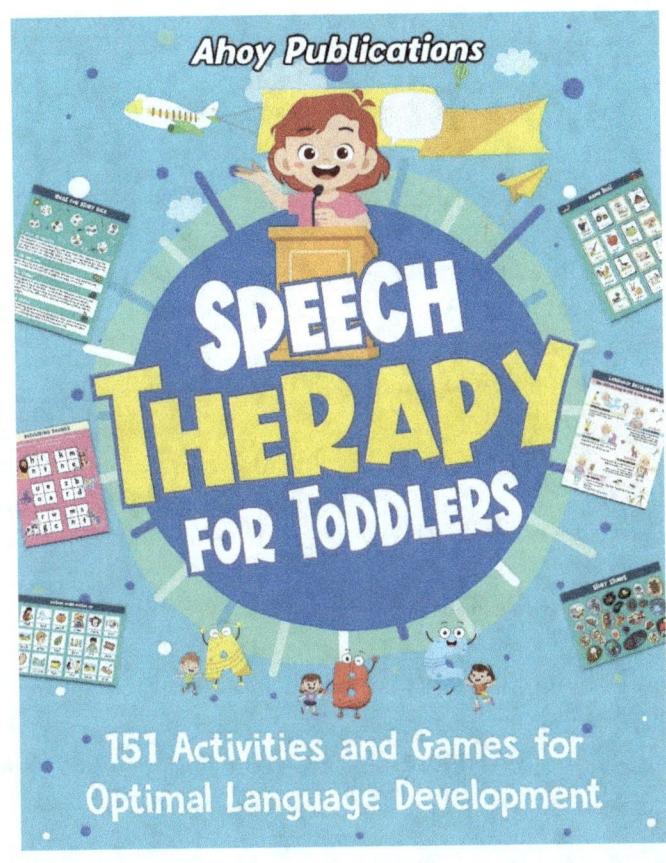

References

(N.d.). Backstage.com. https://www.backstage.com/magazine/article/great-acting-games-for-kids-73608/

(N.d.). Nih.gov. https://www.nimh.nih.gov/health/publications/the-teen-brain-7-things-to-know#:~:text=Although%20the%20brain%20stops%20growing,the%20last%20parts%20to%20mature.

25 easy crafts for toddlers (craft ideas for 2-4 year Olds). (2023, January 9). Craftulate. https://craftulate.com/crafts-for-toddlers/

5 benefits of dance for early childhood development. (2021, June 2). Jooki. https://blog.jooki.com/5-benefits-of-dance-for-early-childhood-development/

6 benefits of preschool performing arts classes for your child. (2022, February 3). Expression City. https://expressioncity.com/6-benefits-of-preschool-performing-arts-classes-for-your-child/

6 fantastic benefits of arts & crafts for kids. (2021, April 4). Tinybeans. https://tinybeans.com/benefits-of-arts-and-crafts-for-kids/

Beck, C. (2022, May 3). Outdoor sensory activities. The OT Toolbox. https://www.theottoolbox.com/outdoor-sensory-diet-activities/

Bergeron, J. (2022, April 1). 20 outdoor sensory play activities for young children + free printable. Active For Life. https://activeforlife.com/20-outdoor-sensory-play-activities/

Breathnach, T. (2020, July 27). 20 amazing things to do outdoors with your preschooler. MadeForMums. https://www.madeformums.com/toddler-and-preschool/20-amazing-things-to-do-outdoors-with-your-pre-schooler/

Browder, A. (2020, February 19). Children are born creative. The Open School | A Self-Directed Democratic School; The Open School. https://www.openschooloc.com/2020/02/19/children-are-born-creative/

Burt, P. (2023, May 4). 30+ arts and crafts ideas for toddlers of 2 and 3 years. Gathered. https://www.gathered.how/arts-crafts/crafts-for-toddlers/

Camille. (2019, April 29). Why Teamwork is Important for Children. Reason Future Tech. https://www.tryreason.com/blog/why-teamwork-is-important-for-children/

Caroline. (2017, September 14). Handprint and footprint baby art project. I Heart Crafty Things. https://iheartcraftythings.com/baby-art-project.html

Cinelli, E. (2022, November 7). 5 quiet activities your child can do instead of napping. Verywell Family. https://www.verywellfamily.com/quiet-time-activities-for-toddlers-6822436

Collage: activity for children 2-6 years. (2022, April 15). Raising Children Network. https://raisingchildren.net.au/guides/activity-guides/making-and-building/collage-activity-for-children-2-6-years

Comments, 0. (2020a, May 13). Egg carton caterpillar craft. My Bored Toddler. https://myboredtoddler.com/egg-carton-caterpillar-craft/

Comments, 0. (2020b, July 17). Butterfly kite toddler craft. My Bored Toddler. https://myboredtoddler.com/butterfly-kite-toddler-craft/

Creating Rhythm ..... A Gift of Love for Your Child. (n.d.). Eblity.com. https://www.eblity.com/special-education-blog/creating-rhythm-a-gift-of-love-for-your-child

Cruz, R. (2022, August 12). 30 cooking activities with toddlers! Teaching Expertise; dontan. https://www.teachingexpertise.com/classroom-ideas/cooking-activities-with-toddlers

Days, S. (2022, March 23). 10 fun cooking activities for toddlers. Sunnydayssunshinecenter.com. https://www.sunnydayssunshinecenter.com/blog/educational-kitchen-activities-toddlers

Della Bitta, A. (2023, April 17). 27 adorable toddler crafts you can pull out anytime. Tinybeans. https://tinybeans.com/arts-and-crafts-for-toddlers/

Dewar, G. (2021, September 11). Evidence-based social skills activities for children and teens (with teaching tips). PARENTING SCIENCE; Gwen Dewar. https://parentingscience.com/social-skills-activities/

Educatall. (2014, May 5). Exploring nature and the outdoors. Educatall. https://www.educatall.com/page/685/Exploring-nature-and-the-outdoors---.html

Erie County Care Management (ECCM). (n.d.). Growing Minds With Cognitive Development Activities for Toddlers. Eccm.Org. https://www.eccm.org/blog/cognitive-development-activities-for-toddlers

Explorers, E. (2019, December 6). 5 Reasons why you should let your child go barefoot. Eco Explorers. https://www.ecoexplorers.com.au/5-reasons-why-you-should-let-your-child-go-barefoot/

Exploring the benefits of sensory play. (n.d.). Goodstart Corporate. https://www.goodstart.org.au/parenting/exploring-the-benefits-of-sensory-play

Five reasons why creativity is important for kids – Studio Jocelyn. (n.d.). Studiojocelyn.Nl. https://www.studiojocelyn.nl/five-reasons-why-creativity-is-important-for-kids/

Garoo, R. (2021, January 27). 23 Best Cognitive Activities For Toddlers Development. MomJunction. https://www.momjunction.com/articles/cognitive-development-activities-for-toddlers_00704930/

Gravenell, A. (n.d.). The many benefits of arts and crafts for children. Kent-teach.com. https://www.kent-teach.com/Blog/post/2021/06/28/the-many-benefits-of-arts-and-crafts-for-children.aspx

Hantak, K., & van der Graaf, V. (n.d.). Why sensory play is important. Communityplaythings.co.uk. https://www.communityplaythings.co.uk/learning-library/articles/the-importance-of-sensory-play

Happiest Baby Staff. (2021, August 12). 6 Low-Fuss Cognitive Activities for Toddlers. Happiest Baby. https://www.happiestbaby.com/blogs/toddler/cognitive-activities-toddlers

How books develop fine motor skills. (n.d.). Babysparks.com. https://babysparks.com/2020/03/09/how-books-develop-fine-motor-skills/

How music and dance can boost your child's confidence and self-esteem. (2023, April 5). SaPa India Blogs; Subramanium Academy of Performing Arts. https://blog.sapaindia.com/how-music-and-dance-can-boost-your-childs-confidence-and-self-esteem/

Hul, J. V. (2022, December 5). How to make blot art hearts. The Artful Parent. https://artfulparent.com/heart-symmetry-painting/

Hul, J. V. (2023a, March 26). How to do watercolor resist crayon art. The Artful Parent. https://artfulparent.com/watercolor-resist-art-with-young-children/

Hul, J. V. (2023b, June 12). 7 simple arts and crafts ideas for toddlers. The Artful Parent. https://artfulparent.com/7-simple-art-activities-for-toddlers

Importance of Art and Craft. (2021, July 20). Classover. https://classover.com/en/blog/importance-of-art-and-craft/

Kids, B. (2019, November 3). The impact of creative play on the brain. The Brain Workshop. https://www.thebrainworkshop.com/blog/the-impact-of-creative-play-on-the-brain/

Kingston, T. (2023, February 12). 75 fun indoor games for kids – boredom busters for all ages. Family Fun Twin Cities. https://www.familyfuntwincities.com/indoor-games-for-kids/

Kitchen science experiments for kids ages 3 to 8. (n.d.). KiwiCo. https://www.kiwico.com/diy/lists/kitchen-science-experiments-for-kids-ages-3-to-8

Kristina. (2021, May 30). Quiet time activities for toddlers and preschoolers. Toddler Approved; Toddler Approved - Simple hands-on activities for busy parents. https://toddlerapproved.com/quiet-time-activities-for-toddlers-and-preschoolers/

Li, P. (2016, December 18). Benefits of sensory play and 21 sensory activities for preschoolers. Parenting For Brain. https://www.parentingforbrain.com/sensory-activities-importance-sensory-play/

Lindner, B. (2019, April 10). Preschool scavenger hunts: Learning through observation. Scholastic.com; Scholastic Parents. https://www.scholastic.com/parents/school-success/learning-toolkit-blog/preschool-scavenger-hunts-learning-through-observation.html

Liz. (2023, June 5). 100+ fun quiet time games and activities for kids. Kids Activities Blog. https://kidsactivitiesblog.com/60561/quiet-time-activities/

London, A. in. (2017, February 23). 15 games & exercises to improve acting skills (taught in drama schools). Acting in London. https://actinginlondon.co.uk/exercises-improve-acting-skills/

Makvana, H. (2015, August 24). 21 fun indoor games for kids aged 3 to 12 years. MomJunction. https://www.momjunction.com/articles/indoor-games-and-kids-activities-for-this-season_00369105/

Marshall-Seslar, A. (2022, January 20). 8 Engaging Cognitive Development Activities for Toddlers. Wellbeingswithalysia.Com. https://wellbeingswithalysia.com/cognitive-development-activities-toddlers/

McClelland, S. (2022, January 31). Salt painting for kids. Little Bins for Little Hands. https://littlebinsforlittlehands.com/salt-painting/

McClelland, S. (2023, July 9). 35 best kitchen science experiments. Little Bins for Little Hands. https://littlebinsforlittlehands.com/4-mini-easiest-kitchen-science-activity-trays/

Mcilroy, T. (2019, May 10). 9 fun music games for kids that are excellent for development. Empowered Parents. https://empoweredparents.co/music-games-for-kids/

Meg. (2023, January 17). 16 (screen-free!) quiet time activities for toddlers. The Toddler Playbook. https://thetoddlerplaybook.com/16-quiet-activity-ideas-for-toddlers-preschoolers/

Michelle. (2023, February 5). Paper crown craft for kids. Taming Little Monsters. https://taminglittlemonsters.com/paper-crown-craft-for-kids/

Miley. (2018, December 14). 10 best improv games for kids. ChildFun. https://www.childfun.com/recommendations/best-improv-games-for-kids/

Millacci, T. S. (2022, January 18). 16 activities to stimulate emotional development in children. Positivepsychology.com. https://positivepsychology.com/emotional-development-activities/

MSU extension. (2017, May 15). MSU Extension. https://www.canr.msu.edu/news/children_and_empathy_teamwork

Occupational Therapy Helping Children. (2023, May 12). Social interaction in play milestones: What you need to know. Occupational Therapy Helping Children. https://occupationaltherapy.com.au/social-interaction-in-play-milestones-what-you-need-to-know/

Ostrosky, M. M., Yang, H.-W., & Stalega, M. (n.d.). Let's get moving: Using children's literature to support physical activity and readiness skills. Eric.ed.gov. https://files.eric.ed.gov/fulltext/ED582061.pdf

Pelly, J. (2020, June 15). Sensory play: 20 great activities for your toddler or preschooler. Healthline. https://www.healthline.com/health/childrens-health/sensory-play

Pieterse, L. (2022, March 30). 25 fantastic improv games for students. Teaching Expertise; dontan. https://www.teachingexpertise.com/classroom-ideas/improv-games/

Playdough activities: children 3-6 years. (2023, May 9). Raising Children Network. https://raisingchildren.net.au/guides/activity-guides/making-and-building/playdough-activities

Pummill, L. (2020, October 21). Patty Case Paper Plate Fish. My Bored Toddler. https://myboredtoddler.com/patty-case-paper-plate-fish/

Pummill, L. (2022, June 29). Paper cup whale. My Bored Toddler. https://myboredtoddler.com/paper-cup-whale/

Pummill, L. (2023, June 16). Fork flower painting. My Bored Toddler. https://myboredtoddler.com/fork-flower-painting/

Reimer, J. (2022, October 30). Preschoolers quiet time activities perfect for 4 year old's - HOAWG. Hands On As We Grow®. https://handsonaswegrow.com/quiet-activities-for-preschoolers/

Sarah. (2022, June 15). 43 Quiet Time activities for 2 year Olds - how wee learn. How Wee Learn - Out of the Box Learning Ideas, Playful Art, Exploring Nature, and Simple Living - That Is How We Learn! https://www.howweelearn.com/quiet-time-activites-2-year-olds/

Shakibaie, S. (2019, March 27). Sensory play: Benefits, ideas & activities. Ready Kids. https://readykids.com.au/sensory-play-for-childhood-development-and-learning/

Sitters.co.uk - the 15 best activities for children to learn through play. (n.d.). Www.sitters.co.uk. https://www.sitters.co.uk/blog/the-15-best-activities-for-children-to-help-them-learn-through-play.aspx

Stockdale, G. (2022, January 15). 6 reasons why art and crafts are so important for child development - ActivityBox. ActivityBox - Learn Creative Thinking the Fun Way; ActivityBox. https://activity-box.com/6-reasons-why-art-and-crafts-are-so-important-for-child-development

Subramani, A. (2020, September 7). Exploring the benefits of sensory play for children. Only About Children. https://www.oac.edu.au/news-views/sensory-play/

Sue. (2021, March 27). 40+ music and movement activities for toddlers and preschoolers. The Montessori-Minded Mom; Reachformontessori.com. https://reachformontessori.com/music-and-movement-activities/

The importance of teamwork for your child - oasis summer day camps. (2022, April 14). Oasischildren.com; Oasis Summer Day Camps. https://oasischildren.com/the-importance-of-teamwork-for-your-child/

Thinking and play: toddlers. (2022, December 20). Raising Children Network. https://raisingchildren.net.au/toddlers/play-learning/play-toddler-development/thinking-play-toddlers

Thompson, T. (2018, January 24). 10 ways to explore nature in winter. Creative Family Fun. https://creativefamilyfun.net/10-ways-to-explore-nature-in-winter/

Tips for keeping infants and toddlers safe: A developmental guide for home visitors – toddlers. (n.d.). ECLKC. https://eclkc.ohs.acf.hhs.gov/safety-practices/article/tips-keeping-infants-toddlers-safe-developmental-guide-home-visitors-toddlers

Today's Parent. (2019, November 12). Best indoor games for kids - today's parent. Today's Parent; SJC Media. https://www.todaysparent.com/toddler/20-fun-indoor-games/

Vanstone, E. (2021, March 11). Kitchen science experiments for kids - 50 awesome experiments. Science Experiments for Kids; Science Sparks. https://www.science-sparks.com/kitchen-science-round-up/

What is sensory play and why is it important? (n.d.). Action for Children. https://www.actionforchildren.org.uk/blog/what-is-sensory-play-and-why-is-it-important/

Why learning through drama is beneficial to child development. (n.d.). The Learning Connections. https://tlc.com.sg/why-learning-through-drama-is-beneficial-to-child-development/

Withers, R. (2019, August 23). Easy yarn suncatchers for kids. The Artful Parent. https://artfulparent.com/easy-yarn-suncatchers-for-kids/

Withers, R. (2022, June 25). Painting with bubble wrap for kids. The Artful Parent. https://artfulparent.com/painting-with-bubble-wrap-for-kids/

Withers, R. (2023, June 14). How to paint with cars: Easy action art for kids. The Artful Parent. https://artfulparent.com/painting-with-wheels-is-fun-action-art-for-kids/